MISCELLANY

**Essays by Young(ish) American Voices
(From the Fringe)**

Miscellany © Run Amok Books, 2018

Individual authors retain all copyrights to their respective works published within this collection.

No part of this publication may be reproduced, distributed, or transmitted in any form or by any means, including photocopying, recording, or other electronic or mechanical methods, without the prior written permission of the author and/or the publisher, except in the case of brief quotations embodied in critical reviews and certain other noncommercial uses permitted by copyright law.

ISBN: 978-1-64255-208-9

Run Amok Books, 2018
First Edition

Printed in the U.S.A.

MISCELLANY:
Essays by Young(Ish) American Voices (From the Fringe)

FOREWORD

This will not be a long or a scholarly introduction, as this collection is intended to be neither of those things. I will not attempt to define the multifarious Modern Essay. Nor will I tightrope across the imaginary and arguably arbitrary line between fiction and nonfiction in order to get a sharper purview of either side, while along the way making the unsteady observation that to me the personal essay seems closer to confessional poetry than nonfiction. These things do not matter. Well, not now. And not here. Those debates can and will be had in other, more appropriate forums. The purpose of this introduction is to simply outline the how and why of the thing: *Miscellany*.

Simply put, a miscellany is mixture of various things; or in this case, a collection of writings on various topics. So why a miscellany? One need only scan the essay section of any e-zine these days to quickly recognize that the range of topics, tones, and even formats of the modern essay is extremely wide and varied. And in fact, that is exactly the *why* of it.

The seeds of this miscellany were planted one afternoon while I flipped (virtually) through the archives of *5x5* magazine and there stumbled upon an essay by Benjamin Woodard, "Exoneration," a 236-word essay in a single serpentine utterance that is both riveting and ominous. Admittedly, at the time, I wondered to myself if this were indeed an essay in the strictest sense of the word.

My appetite now aptly whetted, I not long after happened upon Jen Fitzgerald's calmly mesmerizing slice(s)-of-life-piece, "None of These Tattoos are Mine," a work that affects in the reader a kind of cumulative profundity with real staying power. I recall marveling at the thematic and structural distance between these two pieces—both creative nonfiction, both essays. Yet even as I marveled at that distance, I sensed that somehow they were closer than I had first imagined, rather than father apart.

Eventually I put my finger on it—that single element which brought these two overtly disparate essays together, made them somehow similar and alike: *voice*. There was something in their voice—the voice of an outsider, a voice that occupies that space beyond the customary and the commonplace in society, a voice that flickers on the dark periphery, beyond the blinding compass of that bonfire that is the mainstream. A voice from the fringe.

So there it began—our search for essays by voices from the fringe, essays that would comprise a miscellany. This entailed scouring e-zines and inviting submissions. With the enthusiastic help of Jen Fitzgerald, we uncovered some gems like "The Nature of the Gowanus" by new(ish) essayist Shafina Ahmed. We also solicited submissions from some of our "old(ish)" favorites, more established authors like Noah Cicero and Corey Mesler. We even reached out to Erik Wennermark for a uniquely American expat perspective—different, yet still rendered in the unmistakable voice of an outsider. All of this was done in the hope of bringing together the sensibilities, experiences, and the aesthetic of young(ish) American essayists in a truly singular voice.

It was a pet project, to be sure. But a worthy project, we believed, and still believe. A tradition that we hope to revive again and again in the years to come. Of course, none of it would have been possible if not for the contributors of this miscellany, if not for their near blind trust in an unknown press. For that we thank them .

- Gary Anderson, Editor
Run Amok Books

Contents

The Nature of the Gowanus - Shafina Ahmed	1
Mexico - Noah Cicero	4
Bellies - Daniel Elder	10
None of These Tattoos Are Mine - Jen Fitzgerald	17
On Being Waked - Jen Fitzgerald	26
Birdsong - by Mark David Goodson	30
The World is Wicked When You Grow Up as a Girl - Sarah Marcus-Donnelly	36
A Long Way from Bunny Theater - Corey Mesler	40
Island of Light, Island of Shadow - Nicholas Powers	44
Brad Beckett: A Eulogy - Matthew Sirois	54
Project Men - Matthew Sirois	59
On Saying Goodbye - Matthew Sirois	63
Occupy Tour Guide - Erik Wennermark	67
AQI-XMAS - Erik Wennermark	70
Arriving in Vietnam: the Gift of the Unfamiliar - Erik Wennermark	72
How to Cross the Street in Saigon (not to be attempted after dark) - Erik Wennermark	74
Fight Privilege - Erik Wennermark	77
I am Willy Wonka - Erik Wennermark	79
Exoneration - Benjamin Woodard	86
Notes to a Turntable - Benjamin Woodard	87
TRANSFORMER / TARNSEMOFR_R - Benjamin Woodard	89
Contributors	95
Acknowledgements	99

The Nature of the Gowanus

Shafina Ahmed

Graffiti white bubble letters ink forest green mesh on chain link fences, framing open lots of bleach white sand, gravel, large stones piled in small mountains, yellow bulldozers sitting quiet with their large claws bowed down, against the ground, limbs resting, waiting for someone,   or something to be built from stone in a shaded area where there is no grass
The F train tracks a slope climbing out from deep rooted tunnels, from dark into light   trains ascend and descend rumbling, screeching blue electricity, small strikes of lightning above rows and rows of brick apartment buildings and glass windows of downtown Brooklyn, titanic icicles dangling from the metal train structures, wind frozen solid, entangled in steel, clinging, hundreds of feet above the sidewalks, dripping strings of gravity and time, there are no birds here
The Freedom Tower a steel blue obelisk spiraling upward into a sleek pyramid, monolith prism catching expressions of the sun, marking the spot of history changing the body of this city, contemplating, prayer, reflection, dagger pointed towards the heavens, center of man's skyline scarred and rebuilt, the background of NYC markings of someone's existence here
the sky bright pale blue-ish gray interrupted by office buildings, water towers, antennas poking through thin flat hazy clouds passing over local streets honking, sirens wailing underneath the iron beams of the Gowanus, metal straight lines triangled, squared, rectangled, manipulated sturdy to hold up a world of weight, buttresses layered behind each other, fanning out,   a featherless wing open stretched , riveted, beveled, sharp bones, there are no natural sounds of mother nature here
sunlight shining on a stone quarry yard with random hills of rough stones & parked cement dump trucks, white backs and orange faces, lifeless, facing piles of dust, rubble, chatter of people on the surface

of the wind, dressing people in winter coats, hats, scarves, boots, gloves, fur lined hoods, Eskimos or modern day wolves, exhaling breath solidifying into smoke, cold on lips pursed and nostrils pale pink puffing smoke out like chimneys, the science of warm molecules, fluid and flexible, meeting solid cold, denser heavier barely moving molecules, elements in their most raw form colliding, melting, fusion, compromise, a shift in matter materializing cold days on breath, water, carbon

The form meeting the formless, a strange language in a landscape cracked open like a prehistoric mammoth ribcage, antediluvian forests and seashores of traders trading oils, silks, spices, songs, dreams lifting metal boned planes to the stars, the first light, the first maps, the first storytellers dying and living all at once, an ancient navigation the law of physics – *energy cannot be created nor destroyed*, evolutions of sunrise-sunset making home in a place of unmoving stone, a wildness breathes here, primal, rhythmic, spiritual, untamed beats here, speaks here, far below the cement and limestone revolving this small world into seasons, cycles of sleep, waves, snowfall, iron ore tools scraping the skies and early evening winter moon hidden in the daylight, Nature will one day reclaim itself here

A thin canal filled with unwelcoming greenish-brown muddy waters cuts through the concrete streets, an artificial artery winding and curving ripples as the wind blows, both sides of the canal housed with industrial buildings, open cement lots, construction yards, steel cargo shipping containers, salvage yards, rusted cranes, abandoned factories, skeletons of a past town of farmers, dreamers tilling earth into steel, bedrock, city, nature was abundant here with resources, people, natives, pioneers still digging big holes in nature looking for her secrets, there are no boats or fish in these waters, there are no trees, no flowers here

Everything here keeps moving, the canal, the cars, the trains, the people, even if things are stone, steel, bolted, rooted, wingless

Everything here can be cut through with water

Everything is here because of water

The canal pushing underneath and past the traffic-jammed Brooklyn Queens Expressway,   cars & trucks arcing high above the horizon, underneath them open waters uncontained, free from the concrete canal, exhaling out into the bay of the Atlantic Ocean, sparkling, shimmering a deep dark ocean blue in the low hanging sun, softening the sky red, pink, orange, blue, gold the Statue of Liberty a small green robed figure rising above rooftops & scaffolding, a gilded torch in the hand of a woman, gleaming an open endless sky where there is water, billboards weathered by pollution, salty ocean winds, the air unfolding life.

Mexico

Noah Cicero

It was the year 2000.

People usually think I'm younger, but I'm not. I was born in 1980, then later on failed kindergarten, which put me a year behind.

I grew up in a field. To the people living there, they would never see the fieldness of their lives, but it was a field. In Ohio, the trees, the forest are everywhere. Europeans came several hundred years ago to Ohio, they cut down the trees, they made steel mills, golf courses, spaces for malls, and places for houses. I guess the people that came to Ohio hundreds of years ago did not like trees. To me, the spaces between the trees are fields. Because an open space with grass and not trees isn't a meadow, man-created open spaces are fields.

I grew up in a field surrounded by other field people. We weren't forest people, we didn't use the forest for food or to build our houses. Like most of America, we imported our food and building materials.

On a sunny Friday in the May of 2000 I graduated high school. On Sunday morning, I left in a 1989 Caprice across America to live at the Grand Canyon. It was a rainy morning, it rained all the way to St. Louis. After I crossed the Mississippi River the rain ceased, the sky became blue, the clouds soft and white. I took that as an omen.

In a bathroom in Nebraska, it said "lost in America" on the wall of a bathroom stall. I stared at it, I felt really happy. I wanted to be lost in America, I wanted America. It is weird, I like to think about myself as a patriot; I've been to 40 states, to many National Parks, read a lot of American literature, I've taken classes on U.S. Constitutional Law, I can name probably all the presidents, I can name many Supreme Court Justices, I love George Jones and Sam Cooke and Selena, but according to right-wing people I'm not a patriot because I don't drive a truck, shoot guns, or have a dog. I don't give a shit what they say, I am America as fuck.

My good friend Jake Levine, who lives in South Korea and translates Korean literature, when he was my young, he wasn't dying to discover America, but the world. He took off for England and Spain at the age of 20. I don't know why he chose that, and I don't know why I chose what I did. It never occurred to be visit other faraway countries in a serious way until my 30s.

In the year 2000 I was really into Jack Kerouac; but I don't remember how I found Jack Kerouac. I don't have any memory of the first time I bought *On the Road* or the initial reading, or how I felt. But I must have felt something, because it really got into me. The adventures of Sal and Dean, I wanted that. I wanted to know what it felt like to drive a car across Kansas and Utah and Arizona, to feel the wind hitting me. To see the restaurants of small towns, with their small town people serving and cooking. I would put the map of America on the floor and stare at it, figuring out how to crisscross my country in a way to see awesome unforgettable things. I wanted the unbelievable; at the age of 19 I wanted to create a life that couldn't be believed, and I wanted to live that unbelievable life. I imagined someone giving my eulogy in 2050 saying "I don't know how Noah did what he did, but it happened, and it was awesome."

When I encounter young people nowadays they are filled full of hope about going to college or vocational school, then attaining a job, then working hard and starting a family. But I didn't have thoughts like that when I was 19. I didn't have hope of having a good life; I knew the world didn't like me, and there was nothing I could do about that. The weird thing was I felt okay with the world and its people, I didn't turn into an enraged punk rocker (I just remembered that in 2000 there were still hippies. There was this Phish-Grateful Dead fanbase that hated society and thought doing as many drugs as possible would somehow be their war against society. They are gone. I saw some in Santa Fe, New Mexico in 2011, but when I went to Oregon in 2014 I didn't even see any there; the hippy has become extinct on the American landscape. I saw some "hippy types" in Salt Lake City in 2015, but they seemed different, like they had moved on and created a new sense of identity.)

There was no hope for a great picket fence life for me, I believed in Don Quixote, there were windmills to attack and many Dulcineas out there in the world, who would run through the night with me.

My life didn't turn out well at the Grand Canyon; after working there for a month I got fired for drinking on the job. I didn't know what to do, I still had $2,500 and that was a lot of money in 2000. I met a guy from New Zealand at the Grand Canyon and went to San Diego to live in a small apartment with him. We got a tiny room in a boarding house on Tenth Street called the Buckner Hotel, a hostel now. We had to share a bathroom, everyone in the Buckner Hotel was nuts. At one point a middle-aged black man and white woman offered me money to have sex with them. There was an older white man that would stay up all night writing theology. The guy who ran the Buckner Hotel would sit in his room all night watching VHS porn loudly. And there was a Muslim black woman from the East Coast who would pray on the roof in front of me while I drank beer and smoked cigarettes. She was also involved in a polygamist marriage, but her husband lived with his first wife across town. He paid for her to have a small room, where she did nothing all day but hang around the Buckner Hotel talking to anyone that would talk to her.

I got a job working as a front-desk clerk in a hotel in downtown San Diego; it was called The Maryland Hotel, it is closed now. The hotel was about 100 years old and was full of ghosts and people living off social security. It was so old it had this mezzanine area where people could sit and drink coffee. No one ever drank coffee there. I stood in that area once and it felt creepy.

I remember there was a woman that get up everyday and sat on the couch and watched the sunrise, she told me she survived cancer and thought everyday was precious, which meant she had to see the sunrise.

I met a guy in the hotel and he told he me he knew about Tijuana and he could show me what real life was like there. I told him, okay.

The first thing we did was go to a brothel on Revolution Street. Revolution is the main tourist street and was absurd in 2000 in terms of crap they would sell to Americans. I don't know what it is like now.

We went into a bar, I picked out a girl and went to a small hotel nearby. I don't remember what this person looked like, but I was very attracted to her, she had beautiful black hair, and was wearing tight pants. We went into the hotel, I gave her the money. She went into the bathroom and took her clothes off, she might have given me a blowjob, I don't remember. Eventually we started having sex and I noticed she kept covering her crotch with her hand. I remembered Brian saying that a lot of the hookers were "jotes," pronounced something like "hota." I'm not sure if this is the word; when I googled I came up with nothing. Well, the prostitute turned out to be transgendered. The word "transgendered" did not exist in 2000, if it did, it wasn't in my vocabulary. We had imperfect ways of describing people back then.

I told the girl "Me gusta jotes" which means "I like transgendered prostitutes." The girl took her hand off her penis and revealed an uncircumcised penis. I sucked it. I remember thinking "This is like a chicken wing." I was having really stupid thoughts. Then I had sex with the lady and cummed, then the lady had sex with me. It was the only time in my life there was a penis in my butt. I must have not enjoyed it very much because I never sought it out again.

After it was over, I left.

Then Brian and me went and bought meth. This is the moment, I have a lot of problems with. I had never really done drugs, I had never cared about doing meth. But I was like "okay." We went to this hooker hotel and bought a room. I remember the room being extremely blue, like this pale weird light color of blue. The walls were bare, the bed was hard, I was covered with sweat. I seriously doubt there was air-conditioning. Brian left and brought back meth. Then he removed the light bulb from the bathroom ceiling and broke it in this really coordinated way with a knife I bought on the street.

We smoked meth.

Why was I smoking meth?

I don't remember going to sleep, I think it was the next day, we went to an apartment complex. It was fucked to me. Everything was broken, the whole apartment complex was in shambles. I can still remember standing on the second story, the walkways to the apartments were outside, not sure how to explain it. I remember children running around, the noise of children never ended.

I don't know what we were doing at this apartment complex.

This is what my memory can maintain:

We met another jote named Boly Goma; she was about 30 and was also on meth. She was dating this little dude, who at one point got beat up. I was fascinated by Boly Goma. How did this meth addicted jote prostitute exist? How did her tiny boyfriend exist? Were they existing the whole time I was existing in Ohio? That my whole timeline coincides with their timeline on this earth. And now I wonder, is Boly Goma still in Mexico? Is Boly Goma still alive? Is her little boyfriend still alive? One time Boly Goma came out of the bathroom naked, with her penis tucked between her legs and she said "Look I am a woman." I looked at her standing there.

At one point it was the middle of the night, I was in an abandoned apartment, with other meth heads. For real, I know this sounds insane, but they had candles lit. We were smoking meth by candle.

At some point I should have felt afraid, but I didn't. I think, at that point in my life, I did not know what danger was; I was just sheltered, maybe I thought my privilege would save me.

At one point I was left alone in a hotel room with a 20-year-old man, about the same age as me. A Mexican kid also into meth, but in a non-voyeuristic fashion. He attacked me for some reason, I don't remember why. I doubt I provoked it. He had no fighting skills. When people have no fighting skills they just kind of roll around hoping for the best, and he was probably malnourished also. I grabbed a light bulb and hit him with it on the head, then opened the door and ran away. I got into a taxi and went to a different neighborhood. I didn't have a t-shirt on, which is fucked; I bought a t-shirt at a convenient store.

Later on I noticed I had a horrible bruise cut thing on my body. I think that guy tried to stab me or I horribly bumped myself while high. I have never figured out which.

I don't know what happened next, but I think I ended up in a hotel room in a tourist part of town.

I remember sitting in the dark of the hotel room, the meth wore off and I realized I had been fired from my job and that I would have to go back to Ohio. It felt really terrible; I had failed at the grand canyon and then I failed in San Diego.

I sat in the dark hotel room holding my switchblade to my stomach. I wanted to kill myself via seppuku. I should win an award for that, achieving that level of fucked.

I decided to stand up, put the switchblade down and walk back to America. I found some Americans walking back, they gave me a ride through the border. Then they dropped me off somewhere in San Diego, but I wasn't home. I hitchhiked in the middle of the night. A beautiful 25-year-old woman picked me up; she was so kind, she told me she had lived in Mexico and understood what had happened. Imagine me, covered in old sweat, year 2000, sitting in her car in a dirty white t-shirt, my eyes bloodshot, like a scared bunny rabbit.

The whole thing seems wild to me. I don't feel like I did that, because I never did anything like that before, and I have never done anything like that after.

I'm seriously sitting in this Starbucks with my hand on my chin staring in a trance, trying to come up with some answer to all this. Like did it change me? Did I actually want to die? Who was the woman who picked me up hitchhiking? Is Boly Goma still alive?

Postscript:

I recently went to Chihuahua City, Mexico for a literary event. Everything was fine, the city was beautiful, clean, the beds and pillows soft. I wonder if the Tijuana I just described even existed, or if it was my sheltered mind projecting things on it.

BELLIES

DANIEL ELDER

I'm not sure just where this belly came from. The one right here, where I used to be, the old skin and bones me. This belly. The one right above the hem of my jeans, straining a bit against what used to be a good fit. This strange new thing. I think it began to grow a few months before the election, but lord knows I've been stress-eating since then. I'm not used to this belly. It is so quite new a thing. It protrudes. It swells. When I eat a big meal, it seems to grow even more. I hold it in my hands and wonder at it.

When I look down in the shower, there it is. Like a new landscape emerging after some tectonic shift. I don't know how to feel about this belly. Sometimes I hate it. Other times I cradle it. I stood in front of the mirror yesterday, naked, turning side to side. Running my hands over my body, a body that I have, to my own astonishment, and through great difficulty, learned to find attractive. But I didn't know what to do with this belly. I sucked it in, held it washboard flat, then let out my breath, and my belly with it. Settling back into this new shape.

I have a belly now.

When I was little, the other boys in the gym locker room took to calling me toothpick. I'm not sure who started it, but it caught on. Little boys don't think. The politics of the locker room unspool with an unkind momentum built on laughter and poise. There is little thought to consequence.

I was already confused about my body. My father had strange ideas about masculinity; he thought himself some sort of manly bear, but moved through life ignorant of, or ignoring, his own delicate femininity. He wanted me to stand broad-shouldered and strong and howl at the moon with him, but I was more comfortable in the tender recesses of my imagination than the hard cut of my shoulder blades.

The locker room was a threatening place. Skin and muscle and penis and confusing hierarchies. I was more than skinny, I was rail thin, you could count my ribs. And when they called me toothpick, the word carried on snickers and laughs, it wrote itself into my body, into my bones. You could feel it etched on my ribcage if you pushed hard enough with your fingers. This body. This skeleton and its ridicule.

I hated this skinny body.

During the Siege of Leningrad during World War Two, in a city running out of food and without any hope of escape, my great grandmother starved herself so that her four daughters would have enough to eat. They made ends meet by scraping wallpaper glue from the tenement walls and turning it into soup. They would add leather belts to the broth for flavoring. By the time they escaped, two and a half years later, my great-grandmother's belly was completely distended from malnourishment, swollen as if pregnant with a fifth daughter.

The family eventually boarded a boat for a perilous crossing on Lake Ladoga, while German fighters strafed and bombed. Other boats exploded into splinters of wood and chunks of charred luggage, but theirs made it through. My great grandmother and her daughters all survived. When the war ended they still lived in poverty, still knew hunger, but her belly returned to its normal shape and size.

Eventually, though, she died of stomach cancer.

For the longest time, after high school, after college, I barely had any lovers. Romance and sex were, for me, things that existed mostly in the mind. I pined but didn't pursue. I spent years and years abandoning my body, hardening my consciousness into a homunculus who built a fortress in my skull, feeding my imagination while taking poor care of the body that carried it around.

I was afraid of sex.

I was afraid of what it meant to touch another human being.

What it meant to be touched.

This ugly, unlovable skeleton, poking through my skin.

My grandmother has a belly of iron. Her doctors think she is a walking marvel, how at 97 years young she lives with cholesterol and blood pressure numbers that would make any medical professional blanche, but still eats whatever she wants. That is, in fact, one of her strategies for survival. The oldest of the four daughters, she must remember the Siege more clearly than any of her sisters could, though she never speaks of it. Her stomach must hold desperate starvation like a muscle memory. Grandma is always cooking. Frying her sacred pancakes in cheap vegetable oil, eating meat and dairy with abandon. Her stomach never flinches.

Two summers ago my mother was in the hospital to undergo an operation to remove a tumor growing off the lining of her lung. Grandma came and visited the hospital with her walker, her eyes bursting with old life. The surgery was very dangerous, and the doctors had warned us there was a chance my mother might not survive. My uncle and sisters and I headed out to lunch and wanted to give the two of them, my mother and grandmother, some time alone. We asked Grandma what she wanted for lunch, what we could bring back for her. She thought a moment, then spoke.

Two hot dogs. With ketchup.

Sex-positive. What a revelation. I was twenty-eight, and I'd begun to whisper to friends I could trust about the lust that ran through my blood. The burning desires that I had squelched for years and years. Dreams of bodies of all kinds, not just the breasts and thighs of women but the jaws and cocks of men. My lover took me to the sex toy shop. She went with me and I bought a toy and over time that toy and my fingers found their rhythm in the tightness of my ass. And it was like a re-centering. Like the homunculus was summoned out of his fortress.

Hey!, screamed my body. I'm still here.

We were like two halves of a self, separated far across a field from one another. My mind, my body. And pleasure was the turn of the key that brought us not just closer together, but that helped me look at my body through new eyes. This skinny body. This bony hip, yes, but.

I lay in bed more often, then. Absorbing myself, my contours, just drifting my fingertips across the country of my skin.

My mother survived her tumor surgery, but after just a few days home recuperating, she had to be rushed back to the hospital. She experienced a rare occurrence: volvulus, a medical event in which a section of her lower intestine quite literally twisted itself into a knot. Her belly swelled unnaturally: my sisters and I stood in the emergency room at two in the morning staring at the mound of it as the doctors medicated her and hatched a plan.

She'd had digestive issues for years at that point. Her whole digestive system always seemed to be in a state of revolt, turning against her at every junction. Many of her favorite foods caused her unimaginable discomfort and had to be cut from her diet completely. And now here we were just past a major chest surgery and she would need to have her intestines stapled to the inside of her abdomen.

I wonder if our family's good and bad bellies alternate generations.

Everything changed the night the dancer took me home with him, I had been frightened of this for so long, frightened that going home with a man, this hidden wish of mine, would mean that I would have to change everything about my life, that it would mean I was gay, and I would have to find new ways of defining a self I had just begun to really understand.

And everything did change, but not in ways which I could have foreseen. Rolling in his sheets, twining our bodies together, I found a passion I had hidden away from myself. The way he worshipped my body, which liberated me to glory in its beauty. This body was capable of so much. Its skinniness wasn't a curse but a boon, not because skinny was good, but just because it was who I was, and I was stunning. Riding him, running my fingers through my hair, every thrust unlocking me further. Men, women, in between and beyond, I wanted them all. I wanted to know them. And I wanted for them to know me.

Not just my mind, but my body. My beautiful, beautiful body.

In 2006, my mother traveled to Russia for the first time since she had left the Soviet Union thirty-two years prior. When she asked if I wanted anything as a souvenir, I told her there was just one thing: a magnificent matryoshka. A nesting doll.

She brought home the biggest matryoshka I'd ever seen. Fourteen individual women stacking neatly one into the next, with red babushka kerchiefs cowled around their heads, purple down the rest of their bodies, and explosions of red and yellow flowers and green leaves covering their chests and their bellies.

I unpacked them, one by one, setting them right beside one another so that I had a sense of sweeping changes, the flux of time, just passing my eyes along their diminishing forms. More and more, small details jumped out at me from the handsomely painted wood. The largest doll had hints of wrinkles around the corners of her eyes, and as the dolls got smaller their faces got smoother and smoother, younger and younger. The bouquet of flowers on the largest doll was smaller on the next doll down, then smaller, then smaller, until the flowers closed up into buds, and the buds shrunk, down to the tiniest of the dolls. She was no larger than the last joint of my pinky finger, smaller even, and she was just a little babe in a red onesie.

As I moved from apartment to apartment, the dolls came with me. I never left them all packed away inside their matriarch, but rather let them all out to breathe. They were like a stress toy for my eyes: sweeping one way and then another, small to big and huge to tiny. Exhalations and inhalations. Their changing faces. Their changing bellies. The flowers that grew in their bodies.

I'm not just my mother's son, tied to the mothers before her. My lineage isn't as neat and organized as a matryoshka. There's my father, too. And I do remember his belly. Though we haven't seen each other in a decade, I remember it. I remember his belly and the story it tells.

When I think of my father, it's often this image that surfaces: We're in a nice hotel room in some far-flung corner of the world, after a long day of museums, perhaps, or he's been having one of his seminars where he's had me working selling his books at the back of the room. Now it's nighttime and he sips whiskey while walking around the hotel room in a t-shirt. A t-shirt, and nothing else.

His strange torpedo cock hangs out from the hem, beneath a crinkly and verdant black bush. He swings it around proudly, free and easy. The t-shirt he wears is tight, and faded, and it rises as he walks, so that his belly slips out more and more. He yawns and stretches, his penis thrust outwards, just announcing itself to the world, which in this case is the hotel room, which means me. He grins at me as he steps his foot up on a bed, baring and glorying in his everything, and takes a swig of his whiskey. He scratches his belly. We are men, he seems to think to himself, and this is what it's all about.

That's another reason I start to build the fortress.

The other night my lover came over. We tumbled and twisted and fucked, sloughing off the political sediment of the week and swimming in each other's bodies instead, each other's muscles, each other's skin, the stories we each hold in our joints and flesh. It's been strange, to get tangled with lovers in this new shape. This belly. I worried for a time that I would have to learn all over again. Learn to love this being, this body. Maybe it would take another thirty years.

And there is a newness here to navigate, but it's okay. It's like the doll I was has been cracked in half and a new form has sprung forth to take its place. The same, but different. Beautiful in new ways. Whatever I am, my belly is too.

My lover and I, we lay spent.

They said, while tracing their fingers over my skin: I like your body.

I smiled, whispered thank you.

And I thought, me too.

Me, too.

None of These Tattoos Are Mine

Jennifer Fitzgerald

"I have already lost touch with a couple of people I used to be."
-Joan Didion

We know from cave paintings that marking the body, ritual scarification, and tattooing have been practiced since ancient times. The need to resist the body's desire to remain pristine is a way of asserting our will over the world. When we are young, our bodies are the borders of our world. As we grow older, our former world begins to resist us as the outer and latter world opens up. We hope to remain entirely ourselves throughout this journey; all our glorious incarnations carried along.

You Can Buy A Piece of Me:

Of course I'm late meeting Jeremy. He lives in Queens for Christ's sake. He's been blowing up my phone like I could get the ferry to move any faster. He doesn't need to know that I was copping with Lola in Spanish Harlem.

"The guy isn't gonna wait much longer Jen, we are already an hour late." He always sounds more sexy when he's mad. I can picture those pale blue eyes just burning up.

"Alright, alright, I'm coming." A few minutes later he picks me up at the train in Sunnyside and we are in his 3000 GT heading to 6th Avenue. I smile that cute smile that always gets him and makes him forget how mad he is.

"I hope he can still take you," he says while pulling into a spot. I'm more concerned with these bags burning a hole in my pocket. The Village Tattoo Shop's neon sign lit up the street. Jeremy was all excited about getting me inked, my first tattoo was gonna match his, a Celtic Trinity with knotting. I was just happy to be getting it for free.

The guy's name was "No," like, the opposite of yes, *No*. He's a Latino guy, huge, like 350 lbs. His teeth could have used some attention but I figured as long as his hands were working, we were just dandy.

I put on my best "nice little white girl" voice and say, "Oh, I am so sorry we are late. It's all my fault! It took forever to get here, I live at the end of Staten Island near Jersey. I hope you don't mind if I use the ladies room before we start?"

No smiles and said, "Of course, it's at the bottom of the steps." I barrel down those steps like a wife meeting her husband come home from the war. I close the door quick behind me and pull out a bag. I decide it's best to just do the whole damn thing since I have no clue how much this is going to hurt. No spikes this time around; makes the relapse a bit easier to swallow. At least I'm not as bad as *last time*. A few sniffs with the trusty straw, flush the toilet for affect and head back up to the needle.

I sit in the chair without a care in the world. "Are you nervous?" No asks me. "Naw," I say nonchalantly and put my feet up. I am wearing my checkered pants and my "too cool for school" bright blue, patent leather Adidas. I feel the dope kicking in. My lids lower a little and there's nowhere in the world more comfortable than this ripped leather chair in this dirty tattoo shop. Even the buzz of that jumping needle can't wear me down.

"Damn girl, you so pale I could use transparent ink and still see it on your skin." No says this while putting the pattern on my ankle. He looks at Jeremy, "This look okay to you man?" Jeremy nods and I don't care that he asked him first. He thinks himself one of those "man's man" type of guys; got to control the situation. I'll give it to him for now; dope makes that easier.

I hardly noticed that we'd started. No looked a little surprised that I didn't even flinch. After the first full hour of that needle hammering my ankle he looked up at me and said, "You must have a high tolerance for pain or something, your man was almost crying after an hour." He chuckled and Jeremy rolled his eyes.

"You wish," he said, then kissed the top of my head. "My girl's tough." Sure, I was tough. Tough like a wounded soldier on a Civil War battle field; morphine jammed into my leg to forget about the missing arm. I try not to nod out, that would set off the alarms for sure.

Three and a half hours later I'm done. I've got a piece of Jeremy on my leg. He likes it that way, I can tell.

OM, SHANTI, SHANTI:

I love yoga, I breathe yoga, I can't get enough yoga. I think I might actually be Hindu. You see, I am not one of those yogis who goes occasionally, thinking that the exercise is great but keep the philosophy to yourself. I am yoga. I am the embodiment of Lord Rama. I take everything very seriously.

"Kathleen, I will take you to get your first tattoo. I will even get one with you." My posture has greatly improved because of "downward facing dog" and I stand exceptionally straight while telling her this.

"What are you going to get?" she asks. What am I going to get? What a ridiculous question. OF COURSE I am going to get the Om symbol, the most holy symbol in the Hindu faith.

"I am getting an Om."

"What's an Um?"

"No, not UM, OM! The yoga symbol." I chant a long, drawn out Om while holding my index and thumb fingers together. She rolls her eyes. "Whatever, you are so weird." By now she is used to her sister's ever-morphing strangeness.

I do some research before receiving my sacred marking. I choose the ankle because Oms are not to be shown off, not to be placed in an always visible spot to be scrutinized by non-believers. Also, symmetry is key and this will offset my Celtic Trinity from years back. Greg will be so impressed. Who is Greg? He is my personal yoga teacher. All serious yogis must have one of these, so naturally I retained his services quickly after our initial meeting at the New Age Health spa in Upstate N.Y. He appeared to be in his 30s; I was surprised to find out he was over 50. My friend and I took one of his classes and I impressed him with my bridge and inverted table. I was the only one in the room agile enough to succeed in this yoga feat. He clapped his hands as I hung like a pot rack and yelled, "Welcome to yoga!" The rest of the class was full of W.A.S.P.s that could barely sit Indian style. My friend and I are going to an Ashram with him in a few weeks.

When I met Greg, I was with John. John turned out to be a dud, and now I am with Mike. He reminds me of Jeremy and Jeremy is someone I can't seem to forget. It is just so hard to find someone as enlightened as me. The fact that Mike is a raging alcoholic makes me doubt his spiritual conviction.

The Om only takes thirty-five minutes to permanently find its home on my body. Kathleen got a Celtic Cross and laughed at herself for being so scared of the anti-climactic pain. I talked myself through the moment of doubt I experienced after seeing it for the first time. *This Om represents a higher self and the Hindu philosophy which will always be a part of you. You are important, Shanti, Shanti.*

A few weeks later, my friend and I meet Greg at his home in Long Island. We will spend the night at his place and then head out to the Ashram early in the morning. I am sure to wear only clothes that will show off my sacred tattoo and therefore my piety. Greg takes us out to all the local bars and clubs. I had just broken up with Mike and planned to reinvent myself at the Ananda Ashram. My reinvention was thus . . .

1st Bar: 2 pints of Guinness
2nd Bar: 1 Pint of Guinness, 1 shot of Jameson, a round of pool.
3rd Bar: 2 Jameson and ginger ale.
4th Bar: Actually a club, 2 Long Island Iced Teas, 3 Kamikaze shots out of my friends boobs.
5th Bar: Also a club, 2 Kamikaze shots, 1 Long Island Iced Tea and a Red Devil shot out of my friend's boobs. I decide it is a good idea to go out to the parking lot, drop my pants 100 feet from a bunch of cops and pee leaning up against a van. I am promptly escorted back to Greg's house in car ride of partial consciousness and browning out.

Greg loves my Om tattoo and tells me so as he pulls off my skirt. My friend is passed out on the floor. In whatever consciousness I can salvage, I think of how spiritual this will be and how I will be united with him as if in some Hindu ritual. My body is an alcohol-saturated temple. I am definitely not being taken advantage of; that would be so *un-yoga* of him.

Quote Me:

I have recently transferred to the College of Staten Island's as an English Writing major. After completing a first draft of a 280 page memoir I decided to leave criminal justice, lose over 20 credits and officially start my training as the future world's best writer. While I had really enjoyed my years at John Jay, the commute was trying and my life's calling was screaming to me from the mountain tops. I was very obviously a writer.

I would jump genres, dazzle with my eloquent prose, and obtain small quirks that would lead people to call me "eccentric" and "interesting." The English award I received after completing grammar school should have indicated my talents a long time ago but I was too concerned with the perils of entering junior high.

Writers are so non-descript. I contemplated having a t-shirt made up so I could be immediately recognized for my genius. But to do so would be boastful and of poor taste, so I began drawing up ideas for a tattoo.

Dave and I have been married for almost a year. He loves that I have two tattoos and wants to get me another.

"I want to get a quill with a drop of ink, over a sword with a drop of blood for the saying 'the quill is mightier than the sword,'" I said to Dave one morning over coffee. I showed him my drawings. "I want it on my wrist."

"Are you sure you want it there?"

"Yes, I want it there. It's my body," I say indignantly.

"I know it's your body, but I wouldn't get a tattoo that you hated because you would be forced to look at it all the time."

"This is what I want. If you don't want to get it for me I will just buy it myself."

He huffed and said, "I didn't say I wouldn't get it for you. I just want you to be sure."

"I am sure."

In some act of divine intervention by the cliché gods, when we got to the shop we found that the design I wanted was too large, so I settled on just a quill. After placing the outline on my wrist the tattoo artist called Dave over to make sure it was ok.

"Yea, it looks good. What do you think Jen?"

I smiled, "I love it. Thank you." The tattoo artist immediately started digging into my skin with the needle. I went into a bit of a daze, staring at the floor because this *hurt*. Like, really hurt. When triggered, the bundle of nerves in a wrist will send pain shooting down the hand, out to the fingers, and back up the arm. I thought, briefly yet fondly, about heroin's numbness.

Nearly an hour later I had what I thought were the markings of a writer. I would no longer have to feel awkward using words like ostentatious, loquacious, and delicatessen.

Pulse of My Heart:

Pregnancy makes you take inventory.

When I was 7 months pregnant I decided to take a break from neurotically cleaning my home to neurotically clean dormant social media and web stuff. I eventually made it to an extremely old MySpace account. Amazed that I remembered the password, I rummaged through friend requests and notifications and then checked my inbox. Then air stopped moving for a moment. There was a message from Jeremy, with a subject of "looking for an old friend." It ended with:

> ... I often wonder how you're doing and if you still think of me when you look at the trinity on the front of your ankle that we got for your b-day. I'm in the Marines now for some time. I'm stationed in Japan. I'm doing very well just doing a lot of training getting ready to go to Afghan. Hit me up. I would love to talk.

We hadn't spoken in years. He had moved in and out of my life like a wraith since we met in rehab when I was 16. What did this mean? Why now when things were so solid? I immediately called a friend who grounds me.

"You will never guess who found me."

"Who?"

"Fucking Jeremy."

"Oh no, how do you feel about that?" she asked cautiously.

"I am shocked but I realize I am finally immune to him. It was crazy to see his pictures and stuff but I am happy where I am."

"Oh, Thank God! I was really worried there for a minute."

I laughed, "Did you seriously think I was going to leave Dave while pregnant for an ex-junkie?"

"I didn't know Jen, I know the history there. I am just glad to hear you say that."

I was completely different than the Jennifer that Jeremy had known. It was the only way I could be from then on.

Sometimes, despite its efforts to remain pristine and infinite, the body falls out of sync with the mind. We normally think of this as the other way around—the mind bucking the body. When the two diverge, no matter whom turned first, there is rebellion and a state of unease. But when the body shifts and creaks and spreads of its own volition, the mind feels distraught. This is part of what it means to be a woman, a betrayal.

The scar from where my daughter was cut out of me will always be raised, long, and bright. My mind is forever altered by the first 13 months of sporadic sleep. My psyche is tethered to her well-being as she was once tethered to me. It is all permanent.

Only 6 months old, she sat on my mother's lap in the tattoo shop. Her chubby fingers groped at a favorite stuffed donkey as the needle vibrated over my skin.

A Chuisle Mo Croi

01·11·10

This was the easiest tattoo to get. Not the pain, but the choice. My body marked itself with a palindrome birthdate, that itself marked an existence that would have come to be regardless of time's flipping and wavering.

One day I will show it to her and hopefully be able to tell her about the others. Maybe I will find the means to explain the ways in which women are marked as they move through stages of life.

It gives me pause to think of the stark contrasts between her first visit to a tattoo parlor and mine.

THE TURN:

All the selves move forward with me. The older I get, the more aware I am of my younger selves. It is like I owe them, like I have to bring them along as awareness blossoms.

Stop changing who you are in hopes of being loved.

I've been so many different people just to survive. Now I am on the tail-end of a large-scale betrayal of self that I partly invited and partly manifested. Things were getting easier, I was forming bonds. I felt understood and thought my labor, my hard work could translate into meaningful relationships. I bent and contorted to be anything other than myself because she had never been worthy of praise. Action, movement, distraction. I got a lesson in the heart's impermanence. I got a lesson in old behaviors. I got a lesson in resilience.

Breathe.

I am becoming myself for the first time by reconciling all the faded representations of me. Or will this be another proto-type? There may never be a final me.

Let life unfold.

Be open to the lesson.

So much of who I am is wrapped up in a community that I become hyper sensitive to its nuances and humanness. When you identify yourself in terms of those around you, your worth is measured by their hands.

Just be yourself entirely and everything else will fall into place.

Be open to possibility that, that person is worthy of love.

I am different from the community of writers with whom I feel creatively connected. I will always be different. It's not their fault, and it is not my fault. When I pretend I am not different, I barely hold on. When I make it abundantly clear that I am different, I am treated as such, intensely.

I thought there would be more people like me here...

Do you know what it is like to go to a famed writer's conference and quite literally be treated like maintenance staff by some fellow attendees because your working class background had the nerve to give you a tactile hold on the world around you?

Do you know what it is like to be interrupted incessantly during a planning meeting so that someone can point out your Staten Island accent? "Aww, you said TAWK!" My voice marks me.

When the observer is ripped from their viewing to be viewed, it is sudden and uncomfortable. When the observer is ripped from their viewing to be reminded that they inhabit a different social *place*, they will either wither or burst violently into bloom.

Do you know what it is like to boil over with the latent rage and lash out—break open? I had my Gatsby moment, my *unforgivable*. It can't be forgiven because I am not yet the self who can apologize for having a breaking point. This truth carries its own scarring.

I can't take back the things that mark me, even when I have marked myself with them. So I will own them. I want to commemorate the publication of my first collection of poetry by getting a cleaver tattoo on my forearm. It is fitting, being that the collection is centered around the Meat Cutters of New York City, but mostly it is fitting because I mean to hack off.

Not every part of me will continue on past this turn. I don't know what is around the corner, but I know who I have to be to get there.

I could give up; I could allow the insecurity and uncertainty to win out. Oh, how easy! I could spend evenings counting all the ways that giving up is better than unabashed confrontation of the self, the history, and the unfortunate realities. I could end every night with a sigh of relief at the choice I had made! Maybe I'd be an engineer or get another bartending job. Life would be happy enough. I could paint or something—seek a new, solitary creative outlet. I could let simplicity be king. But then quickly, I deny myself even the luxury of a cop-out train of thought. That is the sort of death I will never be willing to die.

On Being Waked

Jennifer Fitzgerald

I withstood the icy cut of wind chill on the coldest day of the year as I walked to the funeral home from my sister's house. My long, black dress coat did little to shield me from frost-stalked air.

The fact that my sister has bought a home within walking distance of Scalia Funeral Home has alleviated any worry about finding a parking spot—a concern-as-guiding-principle for Staten Islanders. The state of parking is a conversational safe harbor, it is always appropriate to discuss how good or bad the parking is. But talking about how bad the traffic was would make you a complainer.

On the short walk through the semi-suburban neighborhood, I became aware of myself, my funeral garb, my steps, aware of taking them and walking toward the body of another person who'd only seen as much life as I had. I became aware of how familiar I was with this funeral parlor. I've been coming to services here for over 20 years of my brief 35 years on earth, and anticipate at least another 20 years of funerals at Scalia's. I know the entrances, the viewing rooms, and even the sneaky back entrance, through the parking lot, straight into a local and long-beloved Irish bar.

I've known the young man being waked for just as long. He died of an overdose, three days prior, on Christmas Day. It was his fourth and fatal overdose in a years'-long struggle with opiates. I've known both him and this place for most of my life.

We are both Staten Island natives, both from Irish Catholic, working-class backgrounds, we each had a bucket-full of siblings, went to some of the same high schools (yes, plural), hung out in the same bars, with the same groups of people, and we had the same drug of choice. It feels strange saying that in the past tense, just as strange as it would to say in the present tense—because I have created such distance between myself, the drug, and it's other current and former users.

I looked for his name as I walked thorough the foyer into the center hall. He was being waked in an upstairs chapel. The smell of lilies hung on the air like curtains. One of the great disadvantages of being Catholic is the immediate association of fresh-cut flowers with death. All bouquets smell like funeral parlors, not the other way around.

I hung my coat on the rack and began the countdown for how long it would take for me to look at the body. It is a stand-off with myself that I engage in at every wake. He was there. It was an open casket. He looked like a version of himself that no one had met. He looked like a version of himself that no one should remember.

It isn't until after I hug his mother, sister, brother, and daughter, look at the photos, and see his yearbook, that I begin to understand just how alike we were—how similar from the outside, looking in. The Irish face among rows of dark-haired Italian kids with names that start with Di and end in vowels.

Finding ways in which I differ from someone has become easier than finding ways in which we are the same; commonality feels dangerous in a time when other people are so unpredictable.

Scanning the attendees for familiar faces, I saw many and could put names to most. For as much as I was an islander, I was not. I had been pushed out and off, was institutionalized, had moved away, had disconnected socially and culturally from my teen years and on. Placed in an opposition to my *home*, I poured my energy into finding and articulating all the ways in which I did not belong, was not a part of because of fundamental, biological differences. And this feeling of being untethered allowed me to drift far, it allowed me to see myself in comparison to people from all over the country, and it allowed me to look back over my shoulder in judgment.

The more I allowed myself to relate with him, the more emotional and confused I became. He was my peer. Why had I been spared this fate? I started to count: in 9 days, it will have been 15 years since I last used heroin. I was the age his daughter is now when I first used heroin. I had used heroin at a time when heroin use was unheard of on Staten Island. I bought my drugs in Brooklyn and Manhattan. He had started using heroin in the heat of an opiate epidemic. I was an exception, he was a number. I was young, he was an adult. He is only two years older than me. My distance from heroin began to collapse—15 years suddenly felt mutable. I am not special. I am no different. I'm a tally mark, a blip, a flash. I see no good reason why I didn't end up in a casket. Why had I been spared this fate?

How much more was this about responsibility than acceptance? We are responsible for our children, especially when they are minors. Responsible parties have to step out of comfortable places, confront realities, and act. The current culture is one in which we are supposed to accept adults for who they are and the choices they make; staunch individualism. And when you are from an Irish American family, the thick and pervasive veil of denial can easily masquerade as accepting the agency of other adults, family or not.

Using the drugs is about opting out—opting out of a social structure from which I had been excised and had never really found a level of authenticity worth fighting to sticking around for.

I managed to hold myself separate from even the other addicts I was in treatment with. Despite this, I was able to connect. I was able to find unconditional love and acceptance. And I was knocked down a few, necessary pegs with some memorable gems:

You're a worthless junky.

You are a pimple on the ass of society.

Another year out there and you'd be a full-time junky whore (if you aren't already)—I'll bet my life on it.

This wasn't cruelty, it was a means of shaking me into my own reality. If I didn't start seeing myself shoulder to shoulder with the other young people in treatment, if I didn't start seeing them as my community, my collective, my kin, my tribe—I would never make the connections necessary to get clean and sober.

Finding commonality became the key to my survival

I pulled this ideology into my body, infused it into my very state of being. But yet, on this newest return to Staten Island, I've placed myself in an oppositional stance. as though, somehow, in this room full of people, I was *the only* one who didn't belong. I sat in the back row, the weight of all possible outcomes heavy on my chest. "This could have been me," I said to my friend, his former wife, the mother of his child. She nodded her head.

"Why was I spared and he wasn't?"

Pulling yourself out of the hole of addiction is about establishing a connection, hearing the stories of other people, and finding yourself in them. It is also about telling your stories and having others find themselves in them. We connect through our stories— narratives with a single origin that branch out into the infinite possibilities of human experience but remaining connected to the origin, always being able to return to the origin. Getting sober is about finding out that we have been connected the whole time.

We are a *we*. Whether we are using, have used, might use later today, have not used in fifteen years, or whether we have never used. We are not separated by geography, we are not separated by socioeconomic class, our families are not delineated, there are no discernable markers to divide us.

This isn't some B-movie about South Boston featuring one or more of the Wahlbergs. This isn't a reverse tally of siblings, of children buried by their mothers. This isn't a check mark next to a line of other check marks on a spreadsheet of opiate-related deaths. This isn't Hollywood swooping in for a PSA. This isn't an abstract— this is us. This is the whole of us, the sunk and the sinking, the ones who've had to opt out, who were preyed upon by profit, the herd circled by indifference— our wallets yanked out of pockets to pay for the final hole as we hit the ground. How many more of us will we let them bury?

Birdsong

Mark David Goodson

My fingers feel frozen on the keyboard. Some SeaTac highway sits beyond the parking lot and cars are roaring on the other side of the divider. It's a 4:30 in the morning kind of dark, the kind where predawn gray first touches the atmosphere.

I was up before the alarm again. There's things I need to write. People are rioting in my imagination, demanding liberation from the dark recesses of my brain. They want out. They want colored: black letters on a white page.

I'm outside of the lobby of this Fairfield Inn, on one of those benches people sit on while they're waiting for an Uber or a shuttle bus to the airport. It was the only quiet place I could find. The Continental Breakfast, lobby, and office are merged into one efficient use of space inside, with a large flat screen television streaming a George Lopez sitcom. This frozen bench will do.

My daughter has the biological clock of a two-year-old still on east coast time. I can't get a sentence or two in before the text message comes, asking me to get her out of the room before she wakes our four year old son.

I'm optimistic, so I put the laptop in sleep mode, believing I'll be back to the page soon.

Not while I'm with my daughter though.

She struts through the lobby in her pajama bottoms, her eyes are groggy, and her hair's a mess of knotted blonde curls.

"Is that off-ees?" Her speech is a miracle of exuberance in the early hour.

"Yes, that's coffee," I said, acknowledging the carafe in the lobby that she's pointing to.

"Yah. That off-ees."

"Yes, that's coffee." I poured myself a cup.

"That's Daddy off-ees?"

"Yes, that's daddy's coffee."

"Yah. That daddy's off-ees." Her brows furrow in toddler certainty. Another mystery solved.

We watch as the Fairfield Inn staff sets up a complimentary continental breakfast. I am figuring if I feed her with a nice big meal, she'll take a good morning nap, and I can resume the story I'm writing. I'm in the middle of a stream of dialog that cannot be stopped, unless by her. She can stop anything. She can stop the world from spinning, and I'd kneel by her side and say, "Yes, that's daddy's coffee," as we both began to disintegrate.

The only other people awake when the breakfast opens at five in the morning are in workout spandex. I cut up my daughter's watermelon—"Yah. That's my watur-melon"—and think about how I don't exercise any more. I don't break into sweat, anyway.

Writing is definitely exercise. It's why I've quit physical exercise for the time being. There's just too much writing to do. Writing leaves me exhausted at the end of the day, just like physical exercise would. I figure when I publish a book I could get back in a normal physical routine. For the time being, while I am young and healthy, writing is my only scheduled exercise. My wife and I both work and we're raising two kids. I really have time for one pursuit. And the commitment that the pursuit of writing requires is taxing enough to make me forego all others—except parenting, I think as I rub a yogurt stain out of my daughter's shirt.

That's why vacations are so important. Resting the body allows my mind to wonder unimpeded. Ideas don't take vacations. So neither does my writing. This upsets those I'm vacationing with, especially my wife, who takes vacations to get away from work. I take vacations to plunge deeper into mine.

I explain to people that I'm no good at resting. When I rest my body, my mind overcompensates; it consumes all that lost energy in a combustion of thoughts. Many of them are thoughts I need to type out in order to stretch and strengthen. Only then do I feel rested. That's when vacations happen for me, at the end of a long writing session where the words are broken down and exhausted and at rest. It is then that the world becomes a luxury, a source of enjoyment.

Then new words come, seeping through the dark underside of my thoughts like water through a sponge. And then I can't rest again until I've squeezed that sponge dry.

Vacations are my prime time to write. Other people can relax, take calm breaths, revel in an unworried mind. It's in this wide open space that I am a shaky mess. I need to unload my mind daily or else it becomes too heavy and I get angry, unruly.

I relax when I'm six paragraphs into something I really care about. I can't just sit on a lawn chair and pretend that my mind is not teething with thought. Ignored, the words would eat me alive from the inside out. Tended to, those words set me free.

Vacations are the best time for words like the best time for lake fishing is at dawn. Finding time is the hard part. No one else, besides my wife, knows that while on vacation, I am in constant vigil for time alone. It is time I find much more easily during regular workday hours. When a routine is set, I bookend my days writing in the morning and reading at night. It's simple. I'm up two hours before anyone else, and I'm up after the kids go to bed. I get just enough sleep to sustain my work and responsibilities and find the satisfaction of taming these notions that charge through my imagination with wild abandon.

On vacations, I deal with the shifting routines of family. It's no longer about a simple bookend. It's about squeezing in a session here, a session there. I may appear the father with the sacrificial spirit, but I am willing to put my daughter down to nap so I can sit with my laptop in the other room for a blissful hour of outpouring.

So while the rest of the family is downstairs enjoying breakfast—my four year old no doubt eating more pancakes than any little body should—I sing "God Only Knows" to my daughter and sway around our room at the Fairfield Inn like I'm on a ballroom dance floor. I may be trying to put her down too early, but there's a chance that because she was up before five, she'll take her first nap before eight. If her eye rubs and staggered steps were any indication, she will.

I rub her back and tiptoe backwards. To my laptop. The only place to sit where she can't see me is in the bathroom, so that's where I go.

I sit on the covered toilet and hope that my daughter will mistake the prattling keys for the sound of rain drops on her sound machine.

No such luck.

"Daddy. Daddy. Daddy!"

Clever girl. She knows I'm feet away. Why sleep when her daddy can cradle her.

I rub her back some more. I say things like, "It's nap time sweetheart."

This time, I take the laptop out of the room. My mom's hotel room is next door and the family is back from breakfast. So I sit at the desk by the single-serve coffee maker in her room and write while they plan the day out. I tell them there are a few things I have to do and I dive back into the conversation between two people who my mind assures me are real.

A few others enter the room. I try to concentrate. But I hear them talking about me, here and there, in the background. The words get interrupted. The words get angry.

Until, "Mark." It's my wife, and she repeats in sing song, "Ma-ark."

I turn around. "Yes?"

"It worked!" She turns to my mom. "Sometimes I can get his attention."

Her tone informs me she was trying to get my attention before then. But when the words are leaving through the keyboard, they are all-demanding. There is no point in trying to get them on page while pretending to listen to someone else. It is one of the last great uni-tasks. Like having sex, it commands my full attention. I don't know a writer who can forge through to the good stuff while notifications buzz or conversations distract.

It's no good explaining to my wife and mother that, while on vacation, my not-for-profit hobby requires a silent room. How could they know that there are worlds in my mind?—worlds that fade into oblivion without the silence that brings them to life. Some of those worlds I will destroy myself, but some will live and will eventually spin beyond my control. The people who inhabit them will develop their own desires and fates.

How do you explain that to someone?

And then, when a four-year-old tornado of emotion, a child demanding of his own uni-tasking attention, charges into the room with a "I need to go potty! I need to go potty!" like the Paul Revere of the Fairfield Inn, how do you turn to your wife and tell her these delicate and endangered imaginary worlds are more important?

You don't. If I make a bold stand to win that battle, I am losing the war. If I can't make a simple compromise then, I can't make the larger compromises of lifestyle I need to later. So long Thursday night writers group. Why win the battle to lose the war?

I help him to the bathroom, advise a young marksman taking aim. We wash our hands and I walk back into the room with a suggestion in mind. Why don't I leave the room to get this done and my wife text me when our daughter gets up from her nap?

This adventure began at 4:30, and it is now 9:15. Anger is clouding the words like a thick fog. I worry if I can ever get to them again. What's worse is I've carved out some time, sure, but where do I find the space? Our light-sleeping daughter is in our room, and my pre-school son now owns our other room.

To the stairwell, Robin.

Everybody must use the elevator, right? On vacation, it is an unwritten rule of relaxing. You don't take the stairs.

In the east stairwell of the SeaTac Fairfield Inn, I discover something else. Kids always use the stairs. What's more, kids play in the stairwell. Apparently, my quiet oasis is their unsupervised playground. Tag, races up the stairs, games of hide-and-seek, the kids swim around me like fish in a river.

I can't hear the voices in my head. It's killing me.

And there was a time when all I ever wanted was to silence those voices. Abilify used to silence them when nothing else could. Back when those voices belonged in a psych ward, and I fueled their cacophony with an ample drug regimen. Now, sober, I wake up early to hear them like one does birdsong. They produce harmonies rather than discord.

This morning, though, the dialog has all but dried up. I can turn to anger, or—or what? It is anger or an explanation. It is anger or the journaling of a mad man on vacation, made more insane by the world that expects his sanity.

It's anger or I continue on my restart page.

I finish the restart page. I turn it into *the thing* I need to write that morning. I exercise the muscle to let the people in their worlds rest a while, to let them know their time will come.

I turn, in that hallway, away from that mute mechanism of routine, and toward the semblance of a coherent thing: a plea, an explanation, a chronicle of a restless vacationer.

I later rename it *Birdsong.*

THE WORLD IS WICKED WHEN YOU GROW UP AS A GIRL

SARAH MARCUS-DONNELLY

[Context warning: sexual assault]

You are a senior at a boarding school for kids who need to "work on their character" when a classmate comes up to you and says that he is concerned because he has been thinking about raping you. He knows that you are a rape survivor.

When you tell three different adult women, two of them say you are overreacting or you misunderstood him or that he has severe Obsessive Compulsive Disorder and encourage you to find some compassion. One of them is outraged. The one who is outraged is young, maybe 22 years old. She is one of the dorm mothers. She says, "This is not okay." She looks you in the eyes.

The next morning, she marches you to the Dean's office where you retell your story, again. You write down what he said. You ask, what will happen to him? You ask, what will happen to him? You ask again, WHAT WILL HAPPEN TO HIM?

Eventually, they send him to a mental-health rehabilitation program for a few weeks, but they say that it wasn't because of your "incident." When he returns to school, he is cured. It's too late for you, though. The night terrors returned immediately. Before you graduate, during your final student evaluation, one of your favorite English teachers says that you have been self-righteous. Your classmates call you a feminazi. You are one of two Jewish people at your school.

You have been taught that you are "bad at boys." Your junior year, the boarding school decides that you have "boy issues" and they put you on "boy restriction." The school is small and your life is small, so each difficult breakup and teenage mistake is painstakingly recorded by a disapproving public, and your latest breakup is found to be particularly distressing because you are so tearful.

"Boy restriction" means that you are not allowed to talk to boys until a group of your peers decides that you are all better. You are supposed to learn these skills with silence. One of the girls on your restriction committee is in love with a boy who is in love with you. You are in love with another girl, or maybe you're not. When she runs away from school, she sneaks back in through your window one night. She steals your roommate's shoes. You think you are doing the right thing when you tell on her, and three days later she calls the dorm pay phone. "How could you?" she asks, sounding far away.

You recognize her desperation and you can feel yourself breaking apart. You hate her for leaving. You wish you had gone with her. You don't know anything anymore. You sit on the picnic bench and watch them watching you.

The school is small and your life is small.

You are at boarding school when you have sex with a boy in the stairwell who is having sex with other girls and lying about it, but you already know that. Over break, when you visited him in Boston, you were determined to see the city. But the only real memory you have is buying mushrooms from the man by the broken swing on the playground. The city was a blur. You almost missed the train. You also remember how you stood naked in front of the full-length mirror in the boy's room. How he held you there and made you look at yourself for the longest time. He made you say, "I'm beautiful." "Look," he pointed, "Say it." He made you like it.

It is your second week at boarding school. It is summer. You wake up screaming and you know this because your roommate tells you so. You cannot breathe and you cannot see and you tell her, after holding it inside of you like a rotting child for months, that he raped you in the back of his car. Your roommate, who believes she is doing the right thing, tells a teacher who calls you into her office and demands that you tell your parents. "You will do it, or I will do it," she says. When she leaves you in the open vestibule with the payphone to call your mother, you are shaking so violently that you have to dial three times. Your mother asks, "Did you use a condom?"

Your family comes to school for a therapy weekend, but they don't call it that, because no one there is a therapist. You are assigned to a group of equally uncomfortable families, mostly students and their guardians, who sit in a big circle in the girl's dorm living room reading the school's "seminar" guidelines with a teacher. A "seminar" is when you share deeply about your own character and your family secrets with a room full of strangers. You are supposed to share your feelings. You are supposed to discover yourself. The guidelines include sharing only from your own experience.

He made you say, 'I'm beautiful.' He made you like it.

You must vow not to complain, explain, intellectualize, nor protect. The first order of business is when that teacher announces your assault to the group of strangers. Your peers and their parents and some of their siblings look at you. "How does that make you feel, Sarah?" She asks your parents how they feel, and your father says, "There you go fucking up again." And, your mother says, "How is this different than anything else you've ever done in your life?" Your chest pounds wildly and the dizziness makes you sick, but you find your way to the door. You get out of that room. They wait a while before someone tries to find you.

You relive this moment so many times that you begin to question its very existence. But, there were witnesses. And while the one boy who stood up for you after you ran out of the room crying died of a heroin overdose a few years later, the other boy who stood up for you still exists. You sometimes see him on Facebook. The two boys tell your family that their reaction is not okay. Your lungs burn, still remembering the running. You couldn't breathe. You ran from the dorm, across the soccer field, and into the trees.

You are a success story. Thirteen years later, the boarding school wants to interview you for a book of alumni profiles celebrating the school. You read through the interview questions, which include describing your school experience and discussing your high points and takeaways. You kindly decline, because you fear that you are perhaps "not the right person" for this particular showcase. Your parents are disappointed that you said no. "Why can't you just talk about the "good things?"

You laugh about it with your husband, because you have made peace in your heart with God, though you won't forget the trauma. You think about all of those small scared hearts beating furiously together. All of the time you spent wondering if there was freedom on the other side, and the moment you realized that once something decays, it is enduringly gone.

A Long Way from Bunny Theater

Corey Mesler

Once upon a time I had a summer of darkness. Maybe you've had a summer of darkness, a time when anxiety and hopelessness overwhelmed you, and you saw absolutely no way out. Mine was like that, the walls closing in, all doors marked "No Exit," with some spicy variations.

A little background to begin. About twenty years ago I began to experience the acute angst of a debility I had been constructing all my life (apparently), which eventually fell under the rubric "agoraphobia;" that is I had developed a heightened fear of leaving my comfortable home. I have written about this extensively and at least one therapist told me to cease writing about it, cease identifying myself as agoraphobic. It is, however, a part of me, and since I write about my favorite subject, myself, a lot, I find myself often writing about this otherworldly enervation I have contracted as if from alien fungi. It seemed to come out of nowhere, but, like many neuroses or phobias, its roots were dark and deep.

Over the course of this long period of discomfort there have been fluctuations in the strength of the demon's power. There are days when I've quaked under my covers, fearful of waking and walking, and there have been days when I've felt the straitjacket loosen and I've walked around the house, around the neighborhood, around the mall, a seemingly free man. This continues to this day. I still am unable to travel and most mornings I am unable to do much outside of the house. It's worse in the mornings because many bad things are: flus, fears, fatalities. Perhaps it's because exiting the strange kingdom of sleep is like swimming back to a world that should be more familiar but suddenly feels otherwise. But the afternoons and evenings have grown more peaceful, and on good days, I can go out to eat with my wife or my oldest friends, The First Friday Boys (aka The Old Guys in Hats). Being able to eat at one of Cooper-Young's many delightful restaurants has been a joy returned to my life, since eating out was one of the first things the demon took from me. I have always loved eating out, a carryover from my childhood when a trip to Krystal's park-and-eat restaurant, or Mark Twain Cafeteria, was one of my chief thrills.

And then there came the summer of darkness, as we came to call it anon. For some reason—there was a trigger of sorts but it seems, in retrospect, as inane as many of the other inane things about this dis-ease—I suddenly couldn't sleep and, when I did manage to drop off, I awakened into the incubus' supremacy: anxiety inside me like that mean little fucker in *Alien*. And I couldn't eat. Everything made me sick to my stomach. I walked around, a stranger to the world. I was lost inside my malady.

At this time, I was under the care of a psychiatrist (one of Memphis' most renowned but I will not print her name here because she is the Wicked Pythoness in our fable) who, among other things, controlled my meds. I was taking three or four different nostrums which were all designed to make me calmer, and to make my short-circuiting nervous system and digestive system kinder. For a while I was in the middle of the great chemistry experiment called Let's Find a Drug Cocktail that Works. With every new medication, there were side effects which would sideline me for days, if not leave me quaking and puking in strident misery. So, when all this came to a head I did what anyone who had a physician would do. I called my psychiatrist. I was in tears. She would not come to the phone. I thought she was on my side. The receptionist, who acted like an obstinate guard dog the way many receptionists do, told me they could find an appointment for me. I was frantic. I could not fathom driving out to Cordova to her office. Surely, she could hear it in my voice. Surely, she had dealt with other patients who felt they were at the end of their tether. I insisted on speaking to my psychiatrist. A huff and then I was put on hold. Many shaky minutes passed and when my doctor came on the phone her voice was as icy as Death's chill hand. She could do nothing for me until I came to the office. I begged for help. I told her I wasn't sleeping or eating. And then she said this: "If you're really that bad go to Lakeside and get some electric shock." I was dumbfounded. I was blindsided by her meanness, her imperial coldness, her lack of compassion. I hung up. I fell down.

My wife picked me up. My wife who is as brave as Achilles, and as steadfast as the pole-star, picked me up. She made me meet her eyes. "We will make this ok," she said. I didn't believe her. I thought this most treacherous thought: my life is over. There seemed to be no escape from the torture of my malady and the person in charge of taking care of me had turned into a gorgon whom I would never see again, except in my nightmares.

So, began a long summer of walking in the yard and talking to Corey in comforting tones, a long summer of seeking distraction and casting far and wide for something—*anything*—that might comfort me. My wife and daughter would just sit next to me and hold my hand for hours. I was shaken. I was pessimistic. I was almost gone.

About this time my daughter had purchased, with money she saved herself, a rabbit and rabbit hutch. She loved that little hare and my wife built a cunning little fenced-in area in our backyard in which it could run around and chew grass the way rabbits do. We put three chairs around that little enclosure and there we would sit after dinner, night after night, watching that rabbit do nothing but rabbit things. And those things, let's admit, were pretty damn cute. Cuteness was not exactly a cure but, for a little while, I almost forgot the straitjacket. We painted in large glowing letters on the wall of our shed (the sign is there still) BUNNY THEATER.

Somehow, I made it through the summer of darkness. With the help of my therapist I found a new doctor, a caring man about whom I could write another essay entitled The Doctor Who Periodically Saves my Life. I was put on kinder, gentler meds. They began to work. I was not stumbling around as much. I was walking with purpose. I was making it into work at the bookstore (it was because of the summer of darkness that I accepted a new phase in my life, what we would call semi-retirement) some days and enjoying the pleasures of holding new books in my hands, hands that weren't shaking as badly.

So, with the love of family, with the aid of a new admixture of medicaments, with the help of the absurdity of Bunny Theater, with kind words from some friends, with a pleasurable marathon of "My Name is Earl," whose humor penetrated the dark carapace under which I was dwelling, I was able to find in myself some inner strength I thought had perished under the 'uncare' of the devil doctor who dismissed me as if she was flinging phlegm from her fingers. Today I still cannot travel, nor can I do much with my mornings except write (not a bad way to fill the hours of your incarceration), but I go out a bit more in the afternoon, and sometimes I go to the movies, or out to eat. Perhaps most importantly, I play pickleball three times a week. I am resigned to this, this curtailed life, and, with everything that's happened to me in the past 25 years, it's not such a bad prison. And, hearing about one of my recent outings, my supportive friend, Rebecca, said this, "You've come a long way from Bunny Theater."

Island of Light, Island of Shadow

Nicholas Powers

"Here's where the hurricane tore off my roof," she pointed upward. We look at exposed wood beams under open sky. "It was horrible," Ruth crossed her arms. "Doors shook. Water came into the house."

Her son tugged on her pant leg and she lifted him. "We hid in the bathroom." Patting his head, she leaned on the balcony to study the island. It was like a furious giant had stomped and clawed the town of Utuado, Puerto Rico. Trees were snapped. Power lines, ripped. Mudslides bled over roads.

"No electricity. No water. All day to get anything done," she said as she rocked her son. "I don't think it's going to get better anytime soon."

Hurricane Maria

The storm fed on heat. Like an angry spirit seeking release, it climbed the sky. Warm. Sluggish. Slow. Hungry for fury. It found more than wind on the ocean. It tasted carbon, the gaseous exhale of civilization.

It fed on the heat spawned by a billion cars and thousands of jets that crossed the planet. Awakened to its power, the storm screamed like a newborn, its 175 mile-per-hour winds lashed waves upon waves.

Hurricane Maria's eye opened, seeing a path. This fury, half made by nature, half by man. It violently spun in space, cursed hot breaths of lightning and storm. She drew darkness over the islands as the poor nailed wood over windows, heard of her immensity and said her name over and over . . . Maria.

New York City

"Are they safe?" I asked.

"I called," Mom said. "But no one picks up the phone." On screen, a NASA video showed a white foamy spiral around a black hole. Like the sky had been unplugged and all the weight and force of the atmosphere drained into the eye.

Everywhere Hurricane Maria passed went dark and then, slowly, photos surfaced. Dominica. Bahamas. Wrecked. Homes like piles of splinters. Roads cracked. Rivers gushed through the center of town. People digging through wreckage.

It churned over the Caribbean until its dark eye slammed into Puerto Rico and then vanished. An eerie quiet followed. No news came from the island. What happened to our family? What happened to Jesus, my mother's first cousin? His wife Yeya? Their kids?

"Mom, did you hear anything?" I asked.

"No one answers," she said again. "They didn't have much."

San Juan

As the JetBlue plane turned to the airport, I saw homes with blue tarps for roofs. Trees stripped of leaves. Warehouses, filled with shipping containers. Huge chunks of torn earth. When the wheels hit the runway, we cheered.

Outside the hot, damp air felt like a childhood memory wrapped on skin. It had been 30 years since I was in Puerto Rico. My family fled long ago. My grandfather ran from an abusive father. My grandmother from rural poverty. He died after I was born, glaucoma blinded him by the time I was a baby. He held me regardless, a new life in old hands.

Grandma and I lived here briefly. I spoke Spanish and chased salamanders up the walls. The jungle was my playground. We left, again for New York. My Spanish faded but the childhood joy glowed like an ember.

Growing up, I learned that Puerto Rico was a colony, its people and land stolen and stolen again. Shame replaced memory. I spat Spanish from my mouth. A gulf opened between who I was and who I am that deepened for three decades until the island was ransacked by a hurricane. I came back to save what I had loved and lost.

Driving around potholes and under dead traffic lights, I saw storm-beaten buildings. The windows looked like bruises. Street signs were folded by the hands of the hurricane.

I found Caritas de Puerto Rico, they welcomed me in, gave me a plate of food and testified to the island's pain. Danny Rojos, a volunteer, shared how a client, a homeless man, lived on the beach. "He ran for safety as the hurricane ripped roofs off," he said, eyes wide and unblinking. "The zinc roofs flew through the air like knives. Even now, he can't sleep. Too traumatized. That's just one story."

The staff said Padre Monserrate could see me. We sat at the table and he talked in measured words. I asked about relief efforts. A hundred people a day came here for food, water and prayer.

"Anyone can come get a meal, water. It was and is still needed. The first days after the hurricane were horrible," he said. "This generation has seen something they've never seen before. They never saw neighbors dying like this. Never saw helicopters having to deliver food. It forced us to care about each other, more." He tapped his cellphone sarcastically. "We've become so individualistic."

He gave me numbers for churches in Arecibo that delivered aid to towns tucked in the island's mountains. I left and in the car, got a text from Pablo Borges, an activist friend. We planned to meet at the To Go food store.

Night had come. San Juan was a city of shadows. Passing car lights showed couples or lone men or families in brief portraits. Generators hummed as gasoline musk mixed with the sea breeze. Under fluorescent-lit stores, people charged cell phones and talked but often stopped and looked into the darkness as if trying to see a future.

Light and shadow took turns between us. Cars passed by, illuminating our faces in mid-sentence. We talked of Puerto Rico. We talked of the weight crushing the island, how the colonial elite had been replaced by a business elite. Anger drove his breath. The beers rose and fell like pendulums in our hands. I parked and met Pablo, young and wiry, a bushy beard under restive eyes. We went into the store.

He grabbed beers and we drank outside as partygoers gathered on the dark sidewalk. Pablo gestured around, "It's a stateless island. It's a shock to my mom's generation, they always thought the feds would take care of them. Corruption? Drugs? The feds would clean it up. Now, they pulled back and we're on our own."

"Electricity has been failing for a long time," he said. "Now this company Whitefish got a multi-million dollar contract to fix our grid and they had only two full-time employees. They'll hire gringos and none of the money is going to stay here. None. The rich are getting richer and the poor are being left behind."

He took a swig. "There's mobilizing going on. Go see Casa Pueblo in Adjuntas, they've been fighting the exploitation of Puerto Rico for 30 years."

Bayamón

"Jesus *y* Yeya," I shouted through the gate. A large woman dressed in a simple gown came from the house. Wincing at stiff knees, she opened it and hugged me. Thirty years apart, crushed by a hug.

She didn't speak much English. I barely had enough Spanish to say my name right. Or ask directions. I had driven up and down Bayamón looking for a house with a large mango tree. By sheer dumb luck, a guy told me I was one street away. Sure enough, I found it.

She showed me the backyard, the mango tree was chopped down to a nub. The hurricane had broken its branches. Debris littered the yard. They had no generator, no electricity, just relentless heat during the day. Yeya leaned on a chair, squeezed my shoulder and repeated, "Terminado. Terminado."

Her voice was tear-choked but she waved the grief away. Jesus, my grandmother's nephew, rolled in on a wheelchair. He had white hair and a stern face. One arm was a twisted claw from a heart attack and he lifted it to hug me. They fed me coffee, crackers and cheese. I told them I was going to the mountains to report on conditions. While they said be careful, I took my phone and dialed mom's number.

Handing it to Jesus, I saw him press it to his ear as if he could bring her right to his side. His voice rose and fell over the years separating them. He gave the phone to Yeya who laughed and talked, her eyes dancing in her face. They tied their lives together again and our family story flickered like Christmas lights.

I had to leave. Jesus pressed a "thank you" deep into me. Yeya held my face and kissed my cheeks. I got in the car and saw Jesus had wheeled himself out to the front porch to watch me go.

Utuado

The muscleman pulled the cables, zipping the shopping cart across the riverbed as a remix of Queen's "We Will Rock You" blasted from truck speakers. A crew from the radio station Magic 97.3 cheered as they caught it. On the other side, families waved on the ledge of a broken bridge. Massive pieces of it lay on the rocks below.

"There's 25 families stranded on the other side," said Zamaris Rodriquez, one of the staff. "No electricity. No water."

We paused whenever the shopping cart wobbled on cables over the river. Rodriquez had a bullhorn and shouted instructions. Across the chasm, the cart wobbled and then was caught by outreaching hands.

"We come to help," she said. "This is the first time a hurricane shut down the whole island. We had no nature left. All the cows and chickens died. What food was under the soil made it but everything else was wiped out."

The house music thumped through the valley. We both bobbed our heads to it. She sheepishly shrugged. "We need to keep our spirits up." The staff got back into the trucks, Puerto Rican flags fluttering on the hoods as they drove off.

On the other side, people took the supplies home. I peered over the ledge at the pieces of broken bridge, immense blocks of concrete that had been snapped and thrown downstream by raging waters. Here in Utuado, the hurricane descended with primeval force. Breaking. Bending. Smashing.

I walked on a road where homes lay dark, trees ripped up; roots exposed like the tendons of a torn limb. Overhead, power lines spooled from poles. Back at the car, I felt the weight of devastation. My chest was tight. The pain on every face poured into my spirit and the body instinctively tightened to keep it from blurring the mind.

Someone shouted. An older man asked why I parked at the abandoned house. I told him I was a reporter with family in Bayamón. He looked me up and down, went back and came out with coffee, cheese and bread. I was stunned by his kindness.

I drove to Utuado's center, parked at the National Guard's office and asked to see the officer in charge. The young men awkwardly pointed at Jorge Nieves, who laughed at his good luck and agreed to talk.

"Everything was destroyed," he said while pulling up a chair for me. "In the first 10 days, we went on 53 missions and found people with injuries. Some needed oxygen but had no electricity. We got them generators. Airlifted them out. Dropped off food. We were working 22-hour days."

I asked him what could have been done better. "The mayor has put security first, health second," he said. "But every day we see more people with medical needs. There's a lot of diabetes." I thought of the cities with no electricity and asked him about Puerto Rico's future.

He looked away, then back at me. "People are leaving, and it's going to make it worse. We're not going to have enough manpower to rebuild. Already, so many on the island are old or disabled or poor."

He asked me where I was staying. I said in my car. He brought me to the kitchen, gave me plates of food wrapped in aluminum and bottles of water.

Driving away, I looked at the mountain where people lived in the dark. Turning on thin roads that coiled tight, I went up, up, up. On the side were wrecked homes and families talking in the street. A few looked at me suspiciously.

I parked and a pot-bellied man walked toward me as he cleaned a knife. He was scared but tried to hide it. I told him I was a reporter. He put away the blade, called to his friends. One of them said, "We have no electricity, no water. Too many people are leaving. If you have money, you go. The poor have to stay."

They pointed to Ruth Montero who lived down the street with two boys. I walked over and she checked me out and waved me in. She gave me a tour of the house as her story, spilled out in one big wave. "Here's where the hurricane tore off my roof," she said. "Doors shook. Water came into the house."

One of her sons came by and she picked him up. "We hid in the bathroom. Afterwards, it was so sad. There were no trees. Mudslides everywhere. No exit. We were out of power. I searched for water. People put pipes in the hillside, drank, showered and did laundry. They're still doing it now."

We looked out from the balcony. Night had fallen. The hills were black mounds under a purple sky. A few lights shone and people walked by like actors on distant stages. Generators hummed under the symphony of coquis, chirping in the gloom. It was a beauty maybe only briefly visible between bouts of hunger and panic.

She lit a candle. "I was thinking of leaving but I don't think I can make it. It's scary to start over. And my parents live next door. But we have to go through a lot to get a little bit of help from the government. The employees at the agency just talk to each other while we wait."

Her youngest son squirmed in her lap. Her older one rode his three-wheeler in circles in the dark. As she talked, the candle flame wavered and the shadows of the family seemed to jump on the walls as if trying to escape.

"We need help. Trump cut Medicare and it's less now. We deserve to be treated like U.S. citizens," she said. I asked what message she wanted to give *The Indypendent's* readers. Staring across the table, she said, "We are suffering."

I got my things to leave, said goodbye, but in the car, I looked at the food from the National Guard and at her moving in the window. Getting out, I brought it to her.

Adjuntas

"Go ahead." Maribel pointed at the switch. "Turn it on." I did and light beamed down. "It's solar-powered." She proudly pointed at the street lamps of Casa Pueblo. "When the hurricane knocked out the electricity, we still had power." I held my hand under the glow. Weightless. Warm. Free. It was like holding the future.

Hours earlier, I woke up in my car's backseat. I saw deep night. Stars scattered like seeds. Each one a bright grain because Utuado had no power, no light. The island had been thrown back into time's abyss.

Driving to Adjuntas was like being in a submarine as my headlights passed over wreckage. Empty homes. Abandoned cars. Sagging power lines. Guardrails washed away. Roads crumbled into a cliff drop. In the absence of people, the nightmare future was more visible. Is this Puerto Rico decades from now? An island too hurricane-battered to live on?

By sunrise, I was in Adjuntas and went to Casa Pueblo's big hall where Maribel showed me a photo of the first meeting in 1980 when one man showed up. The next time they threw a party and hundreds came. Casa Pueblo united the people to stop a strip mine that would have stabbed the earth. Then a pipeline that could have spilled poison. Now they drove trucks to nearby towns handing out water and food.

"We want to build more," Maribel said of the prototype street lamp. "Make an industry for the people to have jobs. We can protect the island from climate change."

Someone called to Maribel. Time to take supplies to the towns.

I followed them as they gave water to families. Tension left people's faces as they took the supplies. Laughter. Smiles. Eyes brightened with relief. I realized this glowing gratitude was everywhere on my trip. Innumerable acts of kindness had scattered love like seeds for a future Puerto Rico. It was as if I had woken from a deep night and saw the people themselves were stars.

Ponce

The beach was empty. Storm debris littered the sand. Here was southern Puerto Rico, where hurricanes hurled wind and water at the land. Here's where I played as a child.

Thirty years. Thirty damn years. I'd been gone too long. I waded into the sea and cupped the water as if it was my own blood, felt each wave as if it was my own heartbeat, breathed in the breeze as if it was my breath. The trees were my bones. The sand, my skin. The leaves, my hair. The island had poured so much into me that it had become my larger body.

I lay on the waves as clouds darkened the sky. They foretold all the other storms to come. How much time do we have before gigantic hurricanes drive everyone to the mainland? Can we strengthen the island? Can we survive a changing Earth?

And aren't millions being forced to ask these questions? Families fled cyclones in Asia. They fled drought in Africa. They fled fires in the American West. The farther they traveled, the more they looked back to the land that was like their own flesh and blood.

Bayamón

"Señora," I called as Yeya walked out and smiled painfully at knees, still sore. She shook her finger at me.

"Señorita," she made a mischievous eye-twinkle. We laughed. Jesus wheeled over. I told them about the bridge, Casa Pueblo and the beach. They listened, catching my glow more than my words. I said it was time to get a generator and that the family could pitch in.

I unfolded cash and asked Jesus to take it. He shook his head. Yeya looked at him knowingly and took it for him. Neighbors came by. Upon learning who I was, they asked, "New York? What are you doing here?" I told them of the trip. And they nodded politely, not wanting to relive their hurricane night.

I got up to leave and Yeya gave me her phone number. Jesus embraced me for a long time as if to say, in case you don't make it back before I die, I love you. She kissed my forehead as if to say, you are my other son.

Hours later, I stood at the airport. One by one passengers showed their ID to the agent, turned and waved goodbye to weeping relatives. My eyes burned wet. My throat locked. I wanted to stay and rebuild the island. But I had a full life waiting for me in New York. When the time came, I held out my ID to the agent too.

The Next Storm

From the plane, I studied the sky and knew the next hurricane was already being spoonfed. The exhaust from this plane and all planes and cars, factories and farms were heating the oceans. In a year, another hurricane season will begin, another angry spirit will spin, slow and blind at first, then faster and faster until its eye opens.

It will careen through the Caribbean, bouncing off islands. It will shriek 100 mile-per-hour plus winds. It will lash homes, blast bridges and blow rivers off course. It will blow human lives off course.

People will stumble into a quiet morning of devastation. And face life or death. Modern civilization has turned the Earth against us. Death is here now. Death is chasing us inland. Death is forcing us from home. Life means a revolution against a system that has been embedded in us for hundreds of years.

We have to make a choice. I leaned close to the window. The shadow of the plane rippled on the clouds.

Brad Beckett: A Eulogy

Matthew Sirois

"God *damn it*, Jesse!" screamed my history teacher, as he kicked over a front-row desk that had remained—like all the front-row desks—unoccupied. His name was Brad Beckett. I always liked to imagine that he was a relative of Samuel Beckett, the playwright, but there were lots of Becketts in New England, and really I had no reason to have made the connection.

Brad Beckett was a histrionic sort of historian, a guy who had been more-than-well-educated, and developed an interest in our region's colonial past that bordered on being unhealthy. He'd written untold and unsung volumes on the subject that gathered silverfish in the basement of the Historical Society. Through poverty, I imagine, Brad Beckett had come to teach Social Studies to a handful of dirty, half-retarded fishermen's kids at our underfunded correctional facility of a middle school in Thomaston, Maine. He fucking hated it, anyone could tell. Anyone, even a sixth-grader, could also tell that the guy hadn't gotten laid in years. "If you don't figure out how to *sit there* and *listen*, Jesse, you're gonna grow up to be a *criminal!* A *criminal*, Jesse!" The spittle was flying out through his patchy neglect-beard and he bounced a Sharpie pen off the whitewashed brickwork. I don't know if this last gesture was intended to punctuate his evaluation of Jesse, but it did leave a clear "." on the wall.

Now, to be fair, there were plenty of ornery teachers slogging through their tenure at that school. Being an adult now, gradually losing hold of my dreams like Indiana Jones hanging over a chasm from a greased rope, I can relate to that brand of internalized nastiness. But Brad Beckett was something else. Brad Beckett scared the shit out of us. He wasn't a mean person—I wouldn't try to frame it like that—not the archetypal curmudgeon that one expects when one is expecting a scary teacher. Mr. Beckett never seemed to harbor any particular malice toward any particular student, and he wasn't given to needless hectoring of young, fragile egos. Rather, he was scary in the way that any large, unpredictable mammal can be scary. From a distance, the man was almost cuddly: a Chewbacca-like Muppet, pieced together from spare Hushpuppies and corduroy blazers and two-hundred pounds of whatever Naugahyde is made of. But walking into fifth-period Social Studies could often feel like creeping up behind an especially nervous horse.

Being an especially nervous kid, I liked Brad Beckett. I liked the way his prolific nasal hairs would capture particles from the stagnant, sixth-grade classroom air and trap them like sea anemones snagging a meal. I liked the way he wrote on the chalkboard using a chalk extender, which was obviously the least-needful invention since the mechanical pencil. I liked the way he gave every lesson via overhead projector, hunkered above the glowing metal box, elucidating salient points with the aforementioned Sharpie. Mr. Beckett would write out a bullet point . . .

- THE EARLY AMERICANS CAME BY WAY OF LAND BRIDGE, NOW BERING SEA

. . . and then he'd talk for a while on that point, describing the Asiatic tribes who'd made this long, dangerous journey, the wooly mammoths they'd hunted to extinction, the ice age which drew back the Arctic waters and made such a bridge possible. All the while doodling macabre prehistoric scenes on the overhead. Slain mammoths, trampled hunters. Dozens of arrows, either in flight or buried within the cartoonish husks of the dead. Mr. Beckett didn't seem to be aware of his own doodling, never made mention of it, never asked if anyone out in Desk Land could do better. It was like having a direct link to the man's furry, violent subconscious.

I liked that.

✣

I had to pick a topic for my Social Studies final, and I chose the St. George River Canal. I don't remember how I landed on that subject specifically, but I'd always been interested in the idea that our town was where it was because of the river. I liked the river. I went sea-bass fishing with my dad on the river. It was a nice river. A hundred and fifty years prior, the townspeople (or whatever) had dug a relatively intricate canal system to ferry lumber and limestone from the forests and quarries, down the river, and into Thomaston harbor for shipment to places where the local white people were less resourceful. A large portion of the original canal system was preserved, in the form of a little-visited state park, just a couple miles from my house. I rode my bike there and did sketches of the stone work, the bridges. I did rubbings of the cast iron plaques on which dates and names were offered as rooting grounds for moss. My mother took me to the Historical Society headquarters down on Water Street and I poured through albums of nickel-plate photographs, stacks of text. I took notes from so many books, but I was especially careful in recording quotes from histories penned, to my shock, by one *Bradley Beckett*. I put all these materials together into a press-packet-style folder, as if I were briefing the President on matters regarding the St. George River Canal. I took it all quite seriously. And I did the cover illustration myself, using colored pencils and glue sticks and my own hand-rendered old-timey font.

Looking back, my favorite part of that project was sitting in the abandoned park, hanging my arm over the edge of a former capitalist embattlement. The eroded architecture of industry. The stones were all giving in to the landscape, you could see the roots of trees grown between them, and the canal was a slow, green carpet of algae. If I disturbed the water just so, with the afternoon sunlight piercing the muck, I could see dozens of tiny eels who now populated this adjunct waterway, shimmying their tiny bodies in the bored water.

They were only little babies.

✽

"*This*," Mr. Beckett held up my contribution, shaking the blue paper folder until I thought it would tear, "is what I'd hoped, foolishly, that all of you might accomplish. *This* is what following an *assignment* means. I hope you're all prepared for a lifetime of flipping burgers and draining septic tanks, because the way I see it, Mr. Sirois is the *only one here* with anything I'd call a 'future' ahead of him!"

Never mind the fact that Brad Beckett had an obvious crush on my mother. And never mind that I was one of just five students to turn in their paper on time. I'm sure that these things had no bearing on the "A+++" that he'd given my project, which even I understood was not a real grade, or the crippling embarrassment he then ladled over me before my astoundingly cynical twelve-year-old peers. I could see the dull gleam in Jesse's eye which meant I was getting creamed later-on during dodge ball. It would be a long time before I dared put any effort into a school paper again.

I was furious with Brad Beckett at the time, though in retrospect I can't say that the incident did much to sink my popularity. I was already well in the red, where friends were concerned. But I didn't forget it—his pedagogically irresponsible championing of my talent. As life went on and dodge ball games grew infrequent, I found myself appreciating what Mr. Beckett did for me that day. It was like he lit a tiny fire, somewhere in the bruised center of my soul (or whatever), and it kept burning in spite of the lazy inclinations which would visit me throughout high school, the period of time that was supposed to be college, and the ambition-murdering strip mall that is modern American adulthood. He implanted some kind of dopamine receptor in my brain that rewards effort, carries Doctor Jones *up* that damned rope and out of the snake pit. It gets me through the poverty, and the rejection letters, and the long days flipping burgers.

❉

My mother called a little while ago, just to shoot the shit. My family and I try to keep up with each-other pretty regular, ever since I moved west. I'm far from the river, the middle school, the eels. I miss those things, and I think my folks can tell, so they try to keep me informed. *So-and-so just had a kid, so-and-so got married. Dave's Diner closed; they're putting up a friggin' Walmart.* That kind of thing. This time, after we got through my niece switching majors, my dad's achy knees postponing the golf season, and my sister's new job in Florida, Mom told me that Brad Beckett had *passed away*. His name floated to the surface of the conversation like a dead fish.

"Are you serious? How old was he?"

"Oh, probably my age. Yeah. Too young."

Mom didn't realize the gravity of the situation, and neither, at that moment, did I. "Huh," I said numbly, like reacting to day-old game highlights. Turned out that Mr. Beckett had succumbed to a rare type of cancer—thyroid or gall bladder or something—the kind of disease that only comes to a healthy-living person after prolonged exposure to self-loathing. He'd never written a best seller, wasn't the Jared Diamond or Tom Brokaw he maybe deserved to be, despite his religious documentation of who we are. His years of service.

It took me a while to process (or whatever.) I went to the UPS center later that day to retrieve a package that the assholes just couldn't seem to deliver to my home. I was waiting in line, hands in pockets as one does, and I happened to see a calendar on the wall featuring inspirational quotes. This month's offering said:

> *There is an invisible red thread which connects all people who are destined to meet.*
>
> - Chinese Proverb

When it was eventually my turn and the clerk had taken my package slip, I asked him, "Have you read that calendar?"

"Oh," he said, following the direction of my index finger. "Yeah. Why?"

"How the fuck is something both *invisible* and *red*?" I questioned, earnestly.

"I don't know, man." He was staring intently at the monitor between us, having just entered my numbers. "Did you order something from Bed, Bath, and Beyond?"

"Yeah, that's me."

I got back home and I milled around and drank a beer. Unpacked my new curtain rods and installed them using the low-torque electric drill I'd bought because it was cheap. The feeling rose within me as I sorted through all this domestic junk. It flared, vengeful, in the quiet room where only my cat was watching. It climbed out of my heart on a greasy rope. It chased bison across a bridge of ice to conquer the Americas.

Project Men

Matthew Sirois

There were three feet of discarded lead pipe stuck in the ground at a slight angle, adorning the lawn like the straw in a Tropicana orange, equidistant from the porch on one side and the lake shore on the other. Gramp stood next to the pipe, carefully contemplating the thing, holding a Bic lighter and a tennis ball. "Maa-chew!" he called, as he saw me walk out of the house. "Come help me with this sonofabitch!"

The family was assembled inside that lake house, drinking and bantering and pulling together a summer meal. Steamed clams and corn, most likely. The house was a work-in-progress former Boy Scout camp where, upon my first visit, I'd had to shit through a hole in a board and was cautioned not to drink the tap water. Gram and Gramp had only recently bought the place, putting his government pension to work on what they had judged to be a sound investment. I like to describe the economic paradigm my grandparents enjoyed during the halcyon days of the early 90's as "halffluent." They had nice-ish cars, they had a small boat, and they had enough kids and grandkids and nephews and nieces to populate the place for holidays spent trying to water-ski and succeeding to drink coolers full of Molsen Ice. I was probably about ten at the time, and I remember these weekend afternoons at the lake as some of the most enjoyable of my childhood. For one thing, as a family, we were always a fun group. A kind of flannel-and-denim decoupage of recovering Catholics and lapsed alcoholics, French Canadian ne'er-do-wells and British ex-patriots, lesbian ice hockey players and their various, ill-behaved dogs. But, more relevant to my story, it was on these occasions that the men-folk of my family, finding themselves brought together and none of them having much experience with leisure, were obliged to concoct some potentially hazardous *project* for the day—lest their calloused hands fall idle. For you see, I come from a race of Project Men.

"Maa-chew!" Gramp called again, and I rallied myself and so did my father. Not, I think, out of any sort of fatherly inclination to protect me from the Air Force mechanic-turned-freelance-engineer that is my grandfather, but out of sheer curiosity. As it turned out, Gramp was amusing himself by launching tennis balls into the air with M-80 firecrackers dropped down a lead tube. For those who don't know, an M-80 is essentially a "fun size" stick of dynamite, and Gramp had picked up a two-pound bag of these waxy little nitroglycerine cylinders up the road at Hussey's General Store where they were sold from a bin alongside the "fun size" Snickers bars and the "fun size" bottles of Jack Daniels.

"Here," said Gramp, as he handed me a blackened tennis ball. Its fuzzy exterior had been largely melted away and a substance which I decided to be 'tennis ball juice' left a tacky residue on my fingers. "Now, soon as I light this sucka, put the ball on the pipe. Be quick."

"What if I'm not quick?" I asked.

"Well, you'll be scratchin' yer ass with the otha hand, that's what!" Project Men.

"Hold on, Bob," my dad interjected. He was examining the workings of this experiment, and wore a dubious look on his sun-reddened face. "What if we put *four* M-80's down the hole? I betcha we could clear the cedar that way." My father had instinctively understood that launching a ball over the nearby cedar tree was the implicit objective. His pyrotechnic reasoning—though completely without precedent—was convincing. If the tennis ball had been a Russian space chimp, it would have bared its teeth and given two anthropomorphic thumbs-up in something resembling approval.

"Well, I guess prob'ly." said Gramp.

"Okay," said Dad.

"Am I gonna blow my hand off?" I asked.

"Probably not," said Dad.

"You bettah not. Gramma'll have my nuts in a sling," said Gramp.

The two men lit their fuses and dropped their four explosives down the mouth of our lawn-cannon. I did as I'd been told, carefully setting the tennis ball over the pipe like a Faberge egg on its mantle stand and then running a good twenty yards away from my Y-chromosomal origins as they stood there, watching the pipe. A couple of seconds passed. Somebody lit a cigarette. And then, a muffled eruption from the pipe.

Bffft.

The tennis ball was little more than a piss-yellow streak as it broke free of gravity's shackles and entered the troposphere at a velocity of roughly Mach-2. Its trajectory ran 80 degrees to perpendicular (of the lawn), punching through the upper canopy of the big cedar and displacing a nesting pair of endangered North-eastern golden finches, effectively decimating the species. At fifty yards above sea level, the tennis ball reached a point of parabolic entropy and began to descend, eventually making an improvised water landing just north of my five-year-old sister who bobbed, unsuspecting, on a *Little Mermaid* flotation device. Two snarling, leash-less pit-bull terriers dove over and through one-another to be the first to retrieve the projectile from the lake as my sister thrashed in terror and a couple female hockey players on the porch yelled, "KEANU! SWAYZE! . . . *GOOD BOYS!*"

It was a fantastic success.

Not every project was so triumphant. There was, for instance, an attempt on my part to parachute from the roof using non-regulation materials, which left me (literally) and everyone else (figuratively) in stitches.

Some projects had a vein of contrarian genius at their core, like the winter we installed a working telephone booth in the middle of the frozen lake. Torn between the desire to go ice fishing and a pending call from his cardiologist, Gramp let Dad and I convince him to split the difference. Many hours and several hundred yards of telephone wire later, we were sitting in the ice shack, pushing our hooks through the eyeballs of tiny bait fish, when the phone rang.

"Bob? It's Dr. Peters on the other line . . ." I heard my grandmother's English lilt, sounding tinny through the frozen receiver in Gramp's hand.

"Well, take a message Heathah!" he said. "I'm ice fishin'!"

And some projects were genuine things of beauty. My dad and I set out to build a treehouse, once. Or maybe I instigated the thing and decided to recruit him, but, being a Project Man, Dad wasn't all that hard to coerce. The treehouse started so simple, just a little pellet-gun sniping platform on the edge of the woods. But after two dozen evenings, post-work and post-school, the two of us feeding off each other's carpentry buzz, pushing each other, we got to stand back and admire the scale-model replica of our *actual* house we'd hung there, fifteen feet above the carpet of autumn leaves.

I'm a father myself, now. As a metal fabricator, laboring six days a week to keep my family sheltered, my life is full of projects. Sometimes feeling the weight of a hammer in my palm will take me back to that treehouse, which long ago collapsed to the forest floor. Sometimes sawing through pipe will remind me of rocketing tennis balls over the lake, though my grandparents have since moved into a condo with restrictions on the casual use of dynamite. Nobody seems rich anymore, and few would I describe as reckless. But then, there's a younger generation just getting their start.

I buy my daughter block sets, sculpting clay, construction paper. I continually add to her LEGO collection, though she's only three years old and has difficulty with the tight-fitting, sharp-cornered bricks. I want us to have projects to share, and for her to develop projects of her own. Much of this is my own nostalgia, I admit. But I've got philosophy, too. Here's a maxim: *Activity is greater than spectatorship.* Here's a theory: When you build or destroy—whether with nails or cordless drills or gasoline or chainsaws—when your brain is driving your hands to work in the service of fun or utility, it is then that you interrogate the very forces which make the world.

If nothing else, it's a decent way to kill an afternoon.

On Saying Goodbye

Matthew Sirois

Part 1: On Being a Jerk

In August 2016, I left Seattle. My home of ten years, the Pacific Ocean, the place where I made countless friends and met my wife and taught myself how to write and became a father and established the beginnings of an artistic career and truly, finally, maybe figured out who the fuck I am. I packed up my assorted pots and pans, books, sweaters, flannels, an elderly cat—not to mention Signe and our daughter, Ramona, whom I didn't "pack" as they are autonomous beings, unlike the cat—and shipped all of them off to western Massachusetts, to a region known as the Pioneer Valley. Or, as the Narragansett people call it, "The Valley of Far Too Many Liberal Arts Colleges."

The problem was, and is, that I've never been good at saying goodbye. I tend to leave workplaces, for instance, with little fanfare—consciously erasing any trace of myself as I exit the back door. My romantic disentanglements have generally been short and sweet, or shorter and not so much. Social engagements are worse: I leave a party the way D.B. Cooper leaves an airplane. Just excuse myself for a quick piss and drop, whistling, into the night. I tell myself this affectation is part of some writerly mystique, like J.D. Salinger disappearing into a shack behind his family home for months on end (he was a jerk) or Norman Mailer stabbing his wife with a pen knife (the word "jerk" is clearly insufficient for describing the likes of Mailer.) My friends, however, don't think of me foremost as a writer. They think of me as Matthew. And Matthew is, more often than he'd like to admit, a jerk.

Part 2: On Death

2014 was, from where I sat, a year full of death.

Signe had just come back from Europe with her Master's degree, I was writing a book, and our general trajectory seemed to be toward adulthood. After two years of long-distance relationship, it took us remarkably little time to get her pregnant. We were following our chosen paths, doing so together, and soon the two of us would be three.

Our home at that time was a derelict, three-story walkup where two of my old work buddies also resided. Like myself, Daniel and Archie were service industry veterans under 35. They'd suffered similar frustrations, entertained similar hopes, and the three of us shared an easy, kickin' it at the bar kind of friendship. I guess we still had a bit of feral, late-20s nervosa to work through, but things were on track. Daniel was instilling himself as a fixture of the Seattle music scene, and Archie's painting career had gained momentum, with shows and commissions regularly coming his way. I was taking classes, doing readings. Everyone felt they were at the beginning of something; even the changeable drafts snaking through our crumbling apartment complex seemed to bear the scent of change.

And then, preceded only by a series of headaches that were easily written off as hangover symptoms, Daniel collapsed at a punk and metal club downtown. Just suddenly hit the floor, laying there among the boot heels and crushed PBR tallboys. When he didn't immediately come-to, somebody called a car and shipped him off to Harborview with a 20 in his hand. Daniel's MRIs later showed an inoperable mass in his brain. He kept his job for a while, but chemo slowed him down, forcing him to move in with a neighbor. She, a mutual friend, soon became his hospice nurse. Daniel eventually swore off his chemotherapy, the drugs only making him sicker and doing nothing to reverse his slow fade from the visual spectrum.

I remember coming home one evening and seeing the whole block strobing with ambulance lights. I was returning from the bar, having read a book alone while Signe worked and Daniel presumably slept and Archie just wasn't around. Upon seeing the ambulance, I thought, "They must be here for Daniel."

I entered cautiously, ready for it, but no: there was Daniel. Feebly standing in the hallway, watching as Archie's body was wheeled past his friends and neighbors. Past me, over the weed-eaten marble steps, and away. Archie's girlfriend had found him in his studio, after two days without contact. The coroner let us know he'd died of heart failure, that he was slightly overweight and that his undiagnosed arrhythmia and so-forth were not uncommon in young, Black men. As if the commonness were meant to temper our feelings of shock, confusion, and singular loss.

About a month later, Daniel was gone, too.

Signe and I began looking for child-friendly living spaces we could afford. Our folks all flew out from the east coast and we threw a shoestring-budget wedding by the sea.

We left that apartment building, with its hangover memories and overall condition of sinkage. I didn't say goodbye to anybody. Neither Archie nor Daniel had a funeral, in keeping with the tradition of those who bank at Payday Loans. Daniel got a rock concert in his honor, a night of noise and body heat where the line between mourning and reveling was crossed and re-crossed repeatedly. Archie got a party at our local dive, standing room only, the proceeds from whiskey and Rolling Rock donated to pay his long, lonely way back to Georgia. To somebody raised on the dour misdirection of Catholic funerals, these consecutive send-offs were like wakes for Lost Boys—memorializing the casualties of Neverland.

I was still coming to terms with the notion that my generation is mortal when my father was diagnosed with cancer. I kept that news away from any upper-level thinking for months. Ramona was born during this time, which conjures up all manner of metaphor regarding diamonds or any shining, immaculate thing that one pulls from the otherwise dark, subterranean miasma of existence. I flew home to Maine, to sit with Dad, to listen to his deep, broad voice, now confused alternately by pain or morphine. I told him, "Hey, Signe's coming with the baby. You'll get to meet your granddaughter."

Dad would end up missing that introduction by a maddeningly significant two days. Just a circumstance of living far from home that was blameless, but caused me a lot of additional grief.

See, with Archie I didn't have a chance. His death was a bolt out of the ether and nobody was prepared for it, not even Archie. But Daniel and I had months, and spent them more-or-less like the months before his collapse. Sure, the idea of departure hung around every conversation. It was on everyone's mind. But whether in fear, or denial, or simple politeness, we avoided the topic. With Dad, too, all talk was rooted strictly in the present. How are you feeling? What do you think of this book? Let's see what's on TV.

In the end, I never actually said goodbye to any of these people. I merely, at some point, and without knowing it, said hello for the last time.

Part 3: On the Universe

Okay, look: If you subtract the movement of the Earth around the Sun, and the movement of the Sun around the super-massive black hole at the center of the Milky Way galaxy, then we are *still* moving through space at *1.3 million miles per hour*. Away from the "Big Bang", and out into the Great Fuck-All.

What this means is that we are never, and won't ever be, in the same place and time for long. Remember reading the words "Fuck-All" just then? Well, that happened *ten thousand, eight hundred and thirty-three miles* from where you are now. I'm not making this up. Everything is constantly departing, and fast.

I can't put a balm on that type of pain; just like the coroner's report, my philosophy offers nothing in the way of condolence. The world is rushing past us, we're rushing past it, and in the presence of all that movement you could easily spend your whole life saying goodbye.

So, I don't.

Occupy Tour Guide

Erik Wennermark

In front of the People's Liberation Army Headquarters in the Admiralty neighborhood of Hong Kong, a jaunty man in his early thirties, wearing black cargo pants held up with suspenders and a multi-pocketed Batman-style utility belt, a blue t-shirt, and a blue trucker hat skipped down the sidewalk. Like a peculiar Pied-Piper, melded with prop-comic Gallagher and Che Guevara, six or seven intent European faces followed behind him. "Occupy Tour?" he asked interested onlookers. "Please join!"

It was just past midnight on the early morning of Day 5 of Occupy Central and in the entranceway of the neighboring Executive Committee Office hundreds of protestors, along with dozens of reporters and cameramen, paced or sat just across a barricade from forty or more well-armed police. The students had given Chief Executive CY Leung a midnight deadline to resign, or they threatened to extend their occupation into government buildings. CY Leung had come in just under the wire by promising a round of consultations between the students and his deputy Carrie Lam—meetings that were later canceled as a result of reportedly triad-led violence against protestors in Causeway Bay and Mong Kok.

Protestors, however, were uncertain about the concession and the situation remained unresolved; many expected a confrontation. One man in a brown jumpsuit adjusted his facemask, goggles, and black motorcycle helmet. Students wrapped their bare arms and legs in plastic film, preparing to ward off pepper spray. A young girl in a black t-shirt and jean shorts distributed more masks from a cardboard box at her feet and had been at it for hours.

"This building on the right is of course the PLA Headquarters, note the red star on top. It has been recently renovated and the lighting below the star is able to display words. Several months ago a message read 'People's Liberation Army' in simplified Chinese characters.

Here and in Taiwan, we use traditional characters. Needless to say, Hong Kongers were not pleased and the message did not last long." An older French couple dressed in safari duds for a walking outing nodded their heads appreciatively.

"There is a tunnel going under Lung Wo Wan road," the guide said, his hand sweeping the length of the street. "Rumored of course," he added with a wink, "so that underwater vehicles can enter and leave the building from the harbor. There is a large parking garage equipped with tanks. The soldiers housed here are from the mainland and can't, or should I say don't, ever leave the compound, though I am told they are allowed one phone call a week home. The PLA building is next to ExCo, the Executive Committee, where CY Leung has his offices. CY Leung who was asked by students to resign tonight, which he didn't, and almost certainly won't, do."

As he continued on in a manic stream about the ExCo and LegCo (the Legislative Committee), his eyes flashed, gloved hands pointing out each detail or dancing at his sides. Breathless, he stopped for a moment to gather his flock. "Ah yes!" he said, struck with an idea. "An Occupy Tour needs an umbrella." And he took one from his back, held with a rope around his torso, and opened it. The shaft of the umbrella he raised above his head was illuminated like a rainbow glow-stick. "Occupy Tour, anyone?"

The French woman asked when he thought the protests would end. "Ah, that's the question isn't it," he replied with a grin. "I'm afraid no one knows the answer to that."

"But aren't they getting smaller?" she continued.

There were mumbles of ascension from the crowd and he seemed slightly chagrined. "No, no, I think they're just spreading out some. There is Admiralty of course, and Causeway Bay and Mong Kok. I hear there are people in TST." Tsim Sha Tsui, a popular shopping and entertainment district in Kowloon. "Tomorrow's a holiday, then Friday, then the weekend. We'll see what happens. Questions, questions, any other questions?"

"What's the tape for?" a young German tourist asked, referring to the masking tape hanging from his belt.

"Oh, this?" the tour guide answered, pleased with the question. "This goes around my gloves. If you get pepper spray on your hands and arms, it's very difficult to get off. I pepper-sprayed myself to test it and my friends were like 'What?' I was screaming!"

The German man seemed pleased with the tour and offered a bag of chocolate in payment. The tour guide gingerly took one and when the German insisted he take more, rubbed his belly and said, "No, no thank you, I've got plenty here."

As the satisfied crowd drifted off, having exhausted their questions, he patted my shoulder, "Man, it was just a couple French tourists and I was like, alright, why not? Occupy Tour! I gotta go meet up with my friends. Look me up on Twitter, alright?" And Bastien, the Occupy tour guide, sheathed his umbrella and danced away into the heaving crowd.

AQI-XMAS

Erik Wennermark

Jingle Bells is on loop in Burger King. And not even the full version but some minute-and-a-half all-chorus hybrid. At first I hardly register the ting tingle amidst the pirate chatter that is Northern-accented Chinese (Arrr Arrr Arrr), but a co-worker points it out and it centers in my eating experience. The fifth time through my spicy chicken sandwich has become so soiled by yuletide I can barely choke it down; fries languish in ketchup wonderland. "Talk about something please," my co-worker says in a conversational lull. "I can't take this anymore." The chemical make-up of flame-broil.

In Dalian, Liaoning, the sky is clear. A couple of weeks ago the AQI (Air Quality Index) reached 500 and beyond (it goes no higher); the sky darkened like a monsoon of particulate matter. We licked oil off the wind. The sky is a foul thing and one is better to stay inside on such a day; my app mandates wearing a mask, forbids jogging, children outside. Each morning while dressing, check the weather—it's cold—check the air—is it breathable?

Q: What do we sacrifice?

A: Everything. [That which is cheap and plastic and fills the checkout aisles of Target and Walmart. That which costs a thousand dollars (marked down with a subsidy from AT&T). That which fits in your pocket or palm. That which is made by workers who write poetry of their despair in a spare ten minutes in a cramped dormitory of a Shenzhen factory. That which suicides.] Check your stocking.

昏黄的灯光下我一再发呆，傻笑

*Under the dull yellow light again I stare blankly, chuckling like an idiot**

For most here (and there) there is no religious significance to Christmas Day; my co-worker, however, will go to an underground church service (he tells me over Burger King)—"the government-sanctioned churches . . . " he trails off, shrugs, grins, eats a chicken finger. My students will shop, call home sheepishly for more money. The man who owns the malls here, Wang Jianlin, is very rich. He just bought a Hollywood studio and plans to further expand his holdings in the U.S. entertainment industry. There is a tree in the lobby of my building, Christmas lights and Chinese lanterns set up in the courtyard.

It used to be that Chinese products made for export had a higher quality than those meant for domestic consumption. This is changing. Chinese consumers have demanded better—they deserve the same as Western consumers, if not more and better. I'd been in a Walmart just a few times before I moved to Dalian; now I buy my groceries there. The lady who weighs the produce has a mutated arm like an extra in a sci-fi film. She swings the bag closed with the mastery of a cowboy and his lariat. Applies the sticker with her teeth. Remember: Mars is for Martians.

For the New Year I'm heading to Beijing. It will be my first visit to the 3000-year-old capital. The air is much worse there. Here at least we have an ocean breeze to periodically push out the pollution. In Beijing, it is trapped. Last year, the sky killed one million.

*Xu Lizhi "Rented Room"

Arriving in Vietnam: the Gift of the Unfamiliar

Erik Wennermark

The airport when I first arrived in Vietnam: a gaggle of well-wishers and taxi-drivers jostled and pushed into each other; to my unfamiliar ears the language a looping cacophony of dying birds and bleating sheep. Dozens tried to gain purchase with elbow and shoulder, enter the front lines, be first to truly see their disembarking loved one. Amidst the throng stood weary faces, necks tilted, one or another with a cigarette drooping from between lips—the smokers were all men, though there were women too—placidly holding signs against their chests. Those from the nicer District 1 hotels printed in large black letters, even with laminate covers: "Welcome to MR AND MRS SIERIDSSONS from CARAVEL," "SHERATON MR WILSON." Others written in marker or thin, barely legible ballpoint on ripped scraps of paper: "Tim," "Mr. Wes...." dissolved into a smear. The air felt heavy and thick, I began to sweat immediately.

"Don't do anything," my father had said, in the only offering of fatherly wisdom he'd given before I left. "You'll be really tired and don't want to get involved with some asshole who's gonna take you for a ride. Just relax and wait for your head to clear a bit, then get an airport cab to take you to the hotel. Make sure it's an airport cab. They'll fuck you, but it won't be so bad and you'll get where you're going."

Staring out the window as the taxi driver maneuvered through hundreds of motorbikes, some carrying three, four people, weaving through the streets like a swarm of insects, each individual motorbike acting as a discrete element in a larger body, opening and closing around each car or truck, spinning and buzzing and honking through each intersection, without regard for any rules of the road that seemed to be natural, but following their own chaotic path and surviving, thriving. The streets full of people even late at night, restaurants set up on sidewalks with dozens of people sitting at low plastic tables on low plastic chairs eating and drinking and talking.

Open air shops lit by glaring fluorescent light, carts with vats of soup parked in front helmed by women wearing pointy hats like in the movies, but it wasn't a movie at all.

The taxi pulled into a narrow alley and stopped in front of a dark storefront with a closed metal gate. A man pushed a cart festooned with what looked like squid; opening the door the smell confirmed they were at least seafood of some variety. The driver lugged the suitcase out of the trunk and said something, motioning with his fist, before he drove away. I stood perplexed for a moment, then following his lead, I banged on the metal and after a long moment it raised with a rattle and I was ushered into the "lobby" of the hotel. A young man had been sleeping on a thin mattress on the floor. He rubbed his eyes and said, "You late." "Sorry," I said. "The flight . . ." "No problem. You check in tomorrow," he said, and handed me the key, before attempting, unhappily, to manage the heavy suitcase up four flights of stairs.

As I write this, I am teased (or bludgeoned) by the unmistakable tang of durian floating down the hall and into my room, or perhaps it's coming from outside (four floors up). Durian is a strange fruit of a taste and smell so pungent and powerful that it is often prohibited in hotels. Fearful of durian's reputation, I had never tried it, begging off immediately whenever it was offered. But then one day I took a chance. To my delight, I discovered it was quite delicious.

How to Cross the Street in Saigon
(Not to Be Attempted After Dark)

Erik Wennermark

1. Don't look both ways. Don't look at all. Close your eyes and imagine ponies. Deer, crabs, clouds, a rainbow. Things that scuttle or trot, loom; appear across the sky, on both sides at once. Embrace this vision of evanescence and apparition. Hold it for a fragment of a moment. Let it go. Remember: there is always another street to cross. Another bridge yet to pull from the mucked sediment of the churning river.

2. Keep your eyes closed. Step forward. Step again. Imagine you are backing away from a ferocious grizzly stalking you upon the Alaskan tundra. Like that except don't move backwards. Like that except don't wave you arms. (Your personal space has shrunk to within an inch of your skin.) Don't shout or curse. Feel the wind on your arm, your cheek, your lips. Taste the heaving smack of a passing rearview. Now is the time to scream.

3. A small child held in her mother's arms is laughing at you. "Phucking tourist," she says and spits a mass of phlegm to the thirsty ground. Her mother grins sheepishly. "Càm ón," you say, thank you. You are glad of your place upon the earth. You are a student, grateful and obedient. Kiss the child's brow. Kiss the mother's palm, her wrist. Kiss the ground; bring the dirt upon your tongue. Take the woman's calloused feet into your soft hands. Bathe and perfume her feet. Life is a blessed event.

4. Try looking left. The sight of 10,000 rushing motos may alarm you. Do not let it. They will be gone soon, only to be replaced by 10,000 more, and more again. Learn to trust. Close your eyes. Step. Turn your head and look. Watch the machines' rapid departure; hear the diminishing putts of 100cc motors; see the men astride pass a cigarette back and forth. Like them, know your ease, yet exist

within yourself. Disregard the delivery truck that has veered into the oncoming lane. It is a figment. This is your time. Step again.

5. When you were a child, your mother would hold your hand as you walked to school, the crunching snow underfoot echoing in the preternatural quiet of the winter morning. She would remove her glove and you your mitten. Your yearning was mad and unknown for the feel of skin, the warmth of blood. You suspected the truth. Your body, your face cold—scarf wrapped tight around your mouth, it caught the condensation of your breath, the dribble of snot from your nose; lips, tongue and teeth caressing the stiffened undulations of frozen cloth. Your fingers grew together, your thumbs sunken. Your hand aches now, searching for her absent touch.

6. You have lost a flip-flop to the melee. Disregard. There are replacements available on every corner, cheaper and hardier than your own. You've had your shots. You are in no immediate danger and have taken out a traveler's insurance policy as a suitable precaution to the unbidden acquisition of tetanus, dengue, and the like. (Any claim you make will be used in a high-stakes grudge match of trash-can basketball—know that your trans-continental whine became a fine shot taken from well beyond the copier. Hear the whoops of celebration.) Take measured even steps to the midpoint of the street with appropriate knowledge that this space too is a construct. Divisor a tool meant for angels and their braying kin. Show no fear. (Do you remember the bear? The tundra?)

7. If you are clipped, pay no heed; cherish your bruise as a mark of life's bounty. You are foolish to complain anyhow: she was a small girl, not going so fast, dark almond eyes flashing a lurid welcome above her Hello Kitty pollution mask.

8. If you have not yet arrived to the other side of the street, return to *Step* 4 substituting "right" for "left" and vice-versa. If safely across the street, move on to *Step* 9. If your wounds are more grievous than originally suspected seek medical attention. A passing moto driver will be happy to give you a lift (for a small fee).

9. There are moments in life when everything crystallizes. Everything seems to make sense again. This, perhaps, is one of those moments. Accept it as you do all things. Individually and with discretion. It too will pass. Like the rushing motos and your most tenderly held dreams, only a hollowed keening will remain. There is no 4 A.M. without regret, only ever less adhesive plasters of denial and repetition. There is only this, until the next: when the next intersection calls and you've walked up and down the block 3 times and still found nowhere to cross. So marooned you stand, hands in pockets, thumbs resting on the paunch of your money belt, staring meekly at your freshly polished shoes.

Fight Privilege

Erik Wennermark

The bouncer who stood blocking the door was a few inches taller and outweighed me by a hundred pounds. I had him sized up pretty good, gotten his superior dimensions, pushing into him as I was, but still hadn't figured him to be a lefty, so when he swung, wordless, he caught me flush. I took it full, hadn't moved an inch, just felt the popping thud travel through my body.

The bar was a Ukrainian place on 2nd Avenue in the East Village. I had never been before, just walked by a thousand times, don't know why we chose it that night. It was the first or second day in three months I hadn't at least sniffed some heroin and I was bitter and sick. I was looking to get shitfaced, at least make my nausea acceptable, take the edge off what was admittedly a mild withdrawal. I'd been weaning myself off slowly for the previous couple of weeks, but still wasn't pleased about having to clean up: my parents were coming into the city a few days hence for my graduation and I was going through a ridiculously extensive job interview process besides.

I guess maybe this, my anger, my displeasure at having to stop heroin because of my parents and a job, my ennui in this life-moment of university graduation, made me rip apart the bar's bathroom, but whatever it was, I did it. Pulled the already creaky stall from the floor, pissed on the piss-stained wall, cracked a cracked mirror. My first mistake was not leaving directly thereafter, but sitting back down to finish my drink, and then having another. My third drink is when the proprietor discovered his annihilated men's room and called the cops and the bouncer blocked the door. Just after, claustrophobic and flushed, when I tried to get out.

The bouncer swung and hit me hard, not as hard as I've ever been hit (I've been hit several times), but damn hard all the same. I didn't go down, just latched onto him trying to avoid more damage, even threw in a couple of kidney shots. After we danced a while he tossed me off, catching me square again: this is when I went to the floor with my hands wrapped around my head. Thank God one of the guys I came with (a former Marine – Oo-rah!), broke the bouncer's nose with a right cross as he lifted a bar stool up over his head to smash it down on me, his face full of snarling message. My friend's shot giving me the space I needed to get back to my feet and engage the three more who jumped in on the bouncer's side: lapdog bar patrons siding with the man after seeing his nose graciously exploded. I got in some decent shots but was mostly taking damage. My nose started to bleed, a cut opened over my eye, the side of my face already throbbed. Somehow, sometime, somebody got merciful and called them off. The fight trickled down and I bled. We waited for the cops.

Maybe here I'll grant I made another mistake by ditching my friends, but I'm still not too sure about that, even these years later; it was all self-preservation and I wasn't exactly in my right mind anyhow. I was walking back to the bathroom I had destroyed to wash some of the blood off my face when I noticed a side door. It went down a short corridor and back out onto the street. I looked back to the bar, ducked my head, and went through as quiet as I could. I heard some yelling behind me and started to run. I ran three long blocks to Avenue A before they stopped chasing. My friends were pretty piqued that I left them to deal with the cops without me—the chief perpetrator of the bathroom incident—but they didn't get busted by pinning it on a breathless, nameless, me. When my parents rolled into town a few days later for the graduation ceremony, my mother cried when she saw my face. My dad just laughed and said, "A southpaw, huh?"

I got the job.

I am Willy Wonka

Erik Wennermark

Amongst thousands of persons, hardly one strives for perfection; and amongst those who have achieved perfection, hardly one knows me in truth.
— Bhagavad Gita 7.3

Who can take a sunrise, sprinkle it in a dew, cover it in chocolate and a miracle or two?
— Leslie Bricusse & Anthony Newley

"Hey Mister, buy from me! Buy from me!"

The kid flashes a Bollywood smile as he leans on the window of the cab stopped at a crooked intersection amidst dozens of other taxis, trucks, scooters, and the occasional moody wandering cow. I inhale the dusty air, the heat, the sounds of horns and coughs and other chattering baby merchants leaning onto other car windows and engage, "What ya got?"

The kid leafs through his stack, thoughtful, trying to decipher what this strange foreign gentleman might be hankering for on a fine Mumbai morning. His hand emerges from its wanderings, sticky talons grasping a Scooby Doo coloring book. I shake my head and he frowns, furrows his brow. Trying again out comes Sponge Bob. Another negative. The third time is a set of cartoon characters I am unfamiliar with. No thanks bud, my coloring is done brand name.

To his credit, he is not dissuaded by my lack of interest in his wares and simply changes tactics.

"Mister, small money, give me small money. Mister, small money."

"Sorry pal."

Okay, last try. "Mister, one chocolate. Only one small chocolate, just one chocolate, only one!"

The look on his face as he makes this last plea makes clear he thinks I am holding some massive quantities of chocolate on my person. He licks his hungry lips as envious eyes reflect me doing a backstroke in a river of chocolate, an army of adoring Oompa Loompas shower my naked chocolate-y body with gumdrops and sundry.

Before the light turns green (not that lights matter all that much here in Mumbai), coloring-book boy is shouldered aside by a slightly older child with packs of breathtakingly shitty plastic toy cars.

"Mister, buy from me! Buy from me! You have chocolate?"

The light changes, the livestock clears, and we move on, dust in my teeth and cardamom in my nose. At the next light, the child hawkers have those big floppy sunglasses that cover a car windshield to keep the interior from getting too hot. Seems like there would be more of a market for that kind of thing.

I wonder how they split up the merchandise: what process is used to determine who gets what shitty plastic piece of Chinese garbage or slightly more useful air freshener or beaded seat cover.

"Hey Raj, check out this new shit we got bro. Mad Pokemon coloring books—this shit will go like hot chapatti. Ignore these Krishna gear grips over here—I'll take those—lousy shit," says Anand dispersing the items for the day's sale. And poor five-year old Raj trusts fourteen-year old Anand and further looks upon the sheer badassery that is the Pokemon coloring book in front of him and the mad rupees that will pile up as the day's potential customers note the same high level of awesomeness. There is not a Mumbai cabbie who could resist Pokemon's lure, nor a sweating tourist crammed in the backseat, his pockets oozing with melted chocolate.

Chewing and chewing all day long

Somebody said, "Bombay is a bird of gold." I suppose they were referring to the huddled masses trekking from across the subcontinent, and world, to find their stardom or riches in Bollywood, Desi pop music, a McDonald's franchise (due to the prohibition on beef seriously enlivening the veg-friendly menu, Indian McDonald's actually has some tasty food), a smartphone store, or a Tata dealership. It's also probably a bird of prey. Few live in the likes of the

Imperial Towers, a gated, guarded community that shoots high to the heavens from the midst of a shanty town; I tried to sneak onto the premises and scope it out thinking I may get a pass from the patrolman, but was shoed away. Wandering backpackers not allowed. Most Mumbaikars live within the cardboard or crumbling brick walls that make up the fetid rooms beneath the tower's shadow.

There are so very many ravens—picking through the trash, picking at a dead carcass of a kitten smooshed into the street, squawking and picking at each other.

It is illegal to slaughter cattle throughout much of India—the cow is holy in Hinduism for its life-sustaining practices, by-products, and relation to the deity Krishna (a cowherd)—there has even been deadly violence at the mere accusation of a cow's harm. As a result, there are many cows wandering the streets. At some point these cows die of natural causes and they fall down in the street or field whereby they are carrion for the vultures. There was an article in the *Times of India* about building an aviary for the vultures of Mumbai. India used to have the largest vulture population in the world but now most of the birds are gone. The decline in the bird population coincides with the introduction of veterinary medicine. The vultures reacted poorly to something given to the cows and the vultures' kidneys failed and the population dwindled. The lack of vultures is causing additional problems for the city's Parsi population.

I ate in a Parsi restaurant and had to look it up. They are Zoroastrians who fled from Iran to India centuries ago, pushed out by the tide of Islam. They've settled comfortably in India, making up another patch in India's vast and varied ethnic and religious tapestry. Zoroastrians believe a human corpse is unclean and therefore cannot be touched by any of the four cardinal elements; in practical terms cannot be buried or burned. The solution is, and always has been, vultures. This is why they want to build an aviary.

WHAT ARE YOU AT GETTING TERRIBLY FAT?

Mumbai is massive. After living in Ho Chi Minh City, Hong Kong, Tokyo, I thought I'd be prepared for any crazy Asian city, but no.

Mumbai is its own thing. The closest comparison I can make is Cairo, but I haven't been there in many years. Memory likens the two however.

There was an Egyptian guy in line getting an Indian SIM (phone) card. I made the comparison of the two cities to him and he nodded approvingly but was probably just being polite. (SIM cards are a bit of a process in Mumbai as there's a lot of security in this town—cell phone security, wifi security—they're not keen on anonymous data transfers—it's still a far superior option to a 2-year contract with Verizon.) He was in his early fifties and casually but smartly dressed for the heat and unattractive errand; he had the great Omar Sharif Arab-accented English. We started chatting and I threw my few remaining Arabic phrases at him—though I didn't count to 100, which I totally can do—and he said he was in town on business. I said I thought Mumbai was a good place for business and he nodded sincerely, acknowledging my throwaway statement with far more weight than it deserved and pleasing me entirely.

"But the food," he grimaced, "I don't like it."

"Really?" I said, somewhat surprised, "I think it's quite good." He shook his head mournfully. "You know," I continued, "I saw a mezza restaurant near my hotel." He raised up, face alerted to the possibility of hummus, tabbouleh, and shish taouk.

"Where is this? Can you tell me please?"

"Sure thing." I smiled, pleased to return the gift the man's compliment had given me a moment before. I fished in my wallet for the card of the hotel and wrote the street name on the back of his Vodaphone India receipt, noted with the word "falafel."

Later that day (near the hotel and falafel), it was utter fucking madness. Motorbikes in Saigon, Cabs and tuk-tuks in Bangkok, ain't got nothing on Mumbai traffic. The Grant Road intersection is the meeting point of perhaps eight distinct roadways and appears to have created a rip in the fabric of the universe filled with chaotic dark matter and honking horns. It's Tokyo's famed Shibuya Crossing without traffic laws or obedient Japanese. Looming overhead is a massive spider-like elevated walkway that nobody uses (but for a lovely vantage) instead just wading into the mass of cars, bikes, busses, trucks, and people, playing Frogger with their lives.

WHY DON'T YOU TRY SIMPLY READING A BOOK?

The National Gallery of Modern Art in Mumbai has most of the big guns of modern/contemporary Indian art: MF Husain, Ram Kumar et al. The missing links are in the branch in Dehli, including my personal favorite Bhupen Khakhar—a curious relegation as Mumbai/Bombay was his birthplace.

I walk through the gallery: boring river/village scenes, deities, before stopping at an FN Souza painting. Souza is the black sheep of the Indian art world; he booked for New York City at a relatively young age and could never quite handle the whole Indian artist persona—robe-wearing guruji—many others seem to cultivate. He was more in the Western mode: drinking, smoking, and womanizing. His work is too. The pieces I see in Mumbai aren't great: messy cubistic imitation, though a Cezanne-updated still life has its merits. I had dinner with FN Souza once in New York. There's an amazing picture of the two of us: both with scraggly beards and unkempt hair but he a frail Indian man in his eighties and me all young NYC in my twenties. At the time I worked at an art gallery specializing in Contemporary South Asian art, mostly Indian. The dinner was in celebration of an auction of some of his paintings; he made a pretty good cut and deigned to dine with us.

My bosses at the gallery often dangled an India trip in front of me for my continued low-wage service, but I split before it ever happened, if it would have; the gallery's now defunct, the bosses finding better wasteful uses for their money. I hadn't made it to India until now. Whenever I told people about my plans for the trip, they invariably said something along the lines of "I hope you find what you're looking for," which annoyed me as it assumed some sort of vision-quest was in the offing. The one-billion people and ancient culture not reason enough. I got some similar lines writing in my moleskin in a Goa bar: next brilliant novel, right mate? (It's not the "Great American novel" in Goa.) Eh, maybe ten years ago. Genius strikes young, hot, and hard; a great novel and the rest of one's life in a desperate attempt to recreate that first strike. At least I am spared the embarrassment.

I did watch *Darjeeling Express* on the plane over; it's cute, but I don't have brothers and can't really relate to the dynamic.

Pampered and spoiled like a Siamese cat

Six police are "working" the reception area. One carefully draws straight lines with a ruler on a page, one after the other. One crosses his arms and looks menacing. One provides a bit of geniality. One fills out a form on recently hand-ruled paper, having carefully, painstakingly clipped mimeograph paper underneath. One hunts and pecks on a computer entering data from the hand-ruled form the previous guy filled out, the first guy having hand-ruled it. Often the guy who takes notes longhand must translate long passages of his (very level) scrawl for the benefit of the guy hunting and pecking on the computer. The menacing guy rearranges chairs, tells me to sit. I ask the genial guy for a toilet. The computer guy goes to lunch. A sign on the wall says, "Rape is an attack in the soul." I can't even fathom being a sexually-assaulted woman and coming to report the crime to this bunch.

My girlfriend's bag was somewhat ingeniously slashed earlier in the day in a crowded market. We had separated in the mass, she felt a tug, dismissed it. I had heard tell of this crime but had certainly never seen it and was even grudgingly impressed with the clean getaway, a straight-razor rip in her canvas tote. The loss was not great—wallet with credit/ATM cards, a little cash, but passport and phone were safe. Main consequence being I served as an ATM for the remainder of the trip. Despite my protestations to the utility of a complaint, she was aggrieved by the loss and wanted to report it; we had a train to catch that evening and I worried we would spend the day in the police station, but perhaps we could get some insurance money with a police report. We went. We sat.

A blonde European tourist came in exasperated. His bag had been stolen and when he had come in the day before to report the crime the police had encouraged him to report it "lost" instead—we were given the same run-around, gotta keep those tourist crime statistics down. After a night of wallowing in resentment he had changed his mind and wished to change his report to "stolen." Sit down, they say. Tell us the story. But I told you many times yesterday. Tell us again. A man he thought was his friend, they had shared a room and travels and companionship the past week, absconded with his stuff. His face was on the hotel's CCTV. Here is the picture from the hotel—the grainy picture of a dark-skinned man. Here is his name. Wait, this is your friend for seven days? Yes yes I told you, I thought he was my friend. You stay together? Yes yes. You stay together in same room? Yes yes. You are "friends?" We were friends. Friends? Friends. What hotel is this? Scowl.

Clearly the police think some buggery was going on and are not pleased; they may have a word with the hotel management; the blonde boy begins to cry.

The computer is broken. The hours-long refrain is, "Five minutes it will be fixed." We are almost certainly going to miss our train. For clarity's sake, I say to my congenitally well-mannered Japanese girlfriend, "Forgive me, but I will be an asshole now." I stand up and start counting in full voice, "ONE, TWO, THREE, FOUR, FIVE." The policemen look at me, shocked by my behavior. "Five minutes, five minutes!" What is this guy doing? I look at my watch and keep counting. The European guy looks at me emptily, swallowed in his loss. I walk over to the desk, still counting, holding our handwritten copy of the list of "missing" items. The scene is confused. I take the official stamp from the desk in front of the menacing man and stamp the page. After a moment's delay, he realizes my trespass and snarls and reaches out to grab me, but we are already out the door and on the way to the train station. Ugly American.

Outside the station a fortune teller sits cross-legged on a cardboard carpet. A green parakeet chirps in a small wooden cage of polished teak. Face up on the cardboard is the five of swords. I look it up later: self-interest, discord. Birds and bats flit on the surface of the dusky sky; sellers, buskers, and beggars chatter.

Exoneration

Benjamin Woodard

Cold, cold, cold, and in the path of the headlights appear twin car seats, nestled between yellow slashes, vacant of children, their mere presence suggesting a bundle of questions, because it isn't every day that expensive, spotless safety devices are found alone in a forlorn parking lot in this haven for insurance workers and drunk soccer parents, this birthplace of Noah Webster, far from the congregation of cars still occupying spaces at the discount supermarket, and the fact is that six months ago a grandfather was robbed here at gunpoint, so bad thoughts are not ridiculous to have when passing through this parcel of over-privileged suburbia, regardless of their ability to distress, for, yes, this is, overall, a rather decent neighborhood, and, yes, it is doubtful any thief would line these contraptions so neatly on the asphalt before jacking a car, and, yes, without flowers or balloons from the plaza's party store, this certainly cannot be a makeshift memorial, but that does not mean a mother or a father isn't right now driving far away from all responsibilities, nor does it make the sight any less disquieting, and it doesn't bring any sense of relief to realize that, as the headlights shift with the turn of a wheel, there are no moral justifications for two car seats to rest silently, alone, in the cold, cold, cold, watching the sky from the shadows, waiting for snow.

Notes to a Turntable

Benjamin Woodard

Part of me wishes I could brag about discovering hip-hop through you, or that R.E.M.'s *Murmur* somehow made its way onto your platter, but that wasn't my childhood. I grew up in a tiny Massachusetts town; most of my albums came from yard sales.

I was the kid who dragged your needle. The one who bounded about and rattled your arm. My love of Kenny Rogers during this period continues to astonish me. Perhaps it was the beard (Santa?), or the cowboy nature of "The Gambler." Do you recall when I sang "Lucille" into a microphone? Or when I dressed in my homemade *Greatest American Hero* costume and flew around the living room to the 7" of "Believe It or Not"? Then, there was the *Masters of the Universe* story record, the lyrics of which I still occasionally warble, 30 years later: "We will fight (fight, fight, fight)/We will win (win, win, win)."

What spelled your doom? The day I brought home *Thriller*, my first cassette? Or did the shiver of death arrive alongside the combo radio/cassette player we unboxed a few months earlier? I can only imagine the feeling: gathering dust, impotent, while "Wanna Be Startin' Somethin'" oozed from the mono speaker of that little, gray, portable box, all treble, no soul.

Maybe we sold you. Maybe we hauled you to the dump. Your ultimate fate remains a mystery. For that, I apologize.

I once again listen to records. A new turntable is nestled within my electronics cabinet, but the magic isn't the same. No matter my immersion, the raw life that those early albums provided cannot be replicated. I remember how my mom's abundant Barry Manilow collection soothed me. I remember feeling the danger of heavy metal while rocking out to my cousin's copy of "Breaking the Law." I remember the nightmares I suffered after spying the cover art to Kiss's *Dynasty* LP. I remember all of these moments, and I can't help but think that a huge chunk of my personality comes from their resonance.

And yet, I crave more.

So I buy another album. I cut free the cellophane wrapping. I drop the needle, crank the volume, close my eyes, and hope for the best.

TRANSFORMER /
TARNSEMOFR_R

Benjamin Woodard

1. Vicious

Against the advice of my high school guidance counselor, who wants me to study something "worthwhile," I move to Boston in September of 1996 to attend art school.

3. Perfect Day

I elect to live on a substance-free floor. It's filled with kids like myself, who don't do drugs, and with addicts trying to stay clean. In my room, I add a photo of my girlfriend, Jen, to the desktop. I splash one cinderblock wall with magazine cutouts of female musicians I crush over—Shirley Manson, Juliana Hatfield, Justine Frischmann—and a second with a poster for the film *Trainspotting*.

With every move, I hum Lou Reed's "Perfect Day," from his 1972 album, *Transformer*. The song, featured in *Trainspotting*, is one of my new favorites, and I keep on purring its tune as I settle into my new home.

8. Wagon Wheel

My roommate Andrew gets to know our neighbors. I tag along to become their friend by proxy. To say I'm typically shy is an understatement.

Most of the action takes place at the Ping-Pong table in the dorm's rec room. I'm horrible; so is everyone else. Enrique, the guard who sits at the front desk, shakes his head at our lack of finesse and fitness. Our group consists of:

1. awkward nerds like myself, and
2. stoners who fell off the wagon immediately after their parents waved goodbye.

Volleys are hard to come by; our effort is spent chasing balls as they bounce down hallways. We don't care. The game is fun enough, and we're all at the same skill level, regardless of artistic ability.

4. Hangin' 'Round

Some nights, I act as designated scribe, writing out every stupid idea a couple of my recent acquaintances fire off after they smoke massive amounts of marijuana. Other nights, I can't process their altered states correctly and wander on my own. It's around this time that I befriend X and her roommate, Y, and we hang out in the lounge and watch television. They're both drug free; sometimes that's enough to make a friend.

5. Walk on the Wild Side

Not only do I taste freedom in Boston, but I imbibe it in an environment that encourages radical experimentation: Intro classes screen films by Stan Brakhage, Maya Deren, Shirley Clarke, and Phil Solomon; early design drops Joseph Cornell into my life; I walk to the Nickelodeon movie theater and buy a ticket to David Cronenberg's *Crash*, rated NC-17, without the box office clerk giving a second look.

Lou Reed once said, "I know my obituary has already been written. And it starts out, '*Doot, di-doot, di-doot...*'" My hometown inspires no art, no sophistication. It is a dead end. Its obituary has already been written, I decide. The city is my home. Then, at a party where I am sober and just about everyone else is high, someone offers the following advice: "Whatever you do, don't ever try heroin." I nod and say OK, yet my head spins at the thought. What have I gotten myself into? Who are these people? My conclusion: I am a square peg, a sheltered kid who needs to start living.

10. I'm So Free

Eventually, I force myself to call the dorm home and it doesn't sound strange. I look forward to Ping-Pong matches, midnight movies, and gallery openings. I talk with Jen every other day (killer long distance fees) and visit her at Mount Holyoke once a month. Still, I'm not sure if this is where I'm meant to exist.

9. New York Telephone Conversation

Hello?

Hi, Ben, it's X.

Hey.

(Long Pause) I was wondering if I could sleep over your place tonight?

Why?

Y's boyfriend is visiting, and I want to give them our room. It's awkward for me to stay, you know?

Oh.

Andrew's away for the weekend, right?

Yeah.

It's just you over there?

Yeah.

You must be bored.

I've got work to keep me busy.

You probably want someone to talk to, right?

What?

You can't work all night.

No, I can't.

We can keep each other company.

7. Satellite of Love

X arrives after eleven, carrying her pillow and a blanket. She's in pajamas, but her face is radiant. We sit on my bed and talk for a while. Her voice is raspy. It gets late. The city outside is so very quiet.

When the time comes, though, I don't make room for X. I don't give X my bed, or Andrew's bed. I ask her to sleep alone on the floor. I am incredibly naïve. This is the last night X stops by my room.

6. Make Up

In his review of *Transformer* for *Rolling Stone* in early 1973, journalist Nick Tosches filleted the song "Make Up," writing, "It isn't decadent, it isn't perverse, it isn't rock & roll." The critiques I receive in class sometimes rival Tosches's assessment. Their words are harsher than I expect. My ideas seem so simple. Nothing breaks through, regardless of my persistence. Who defines rock & roll, I wonder?

I spend so much time carefully navigating the line of acceptability at art school, both in my work and my developing persona. Because of this, the desire to be surrounded by other artists in the big city, which sounded so lovely back in high school, weighs on my shoulders.

2. Andy's Chest

Andrew resolves to shoot a short film near the end of the semester. I help out and set up lights. In one scene, he convinces the guy across the hall, a total live wire, to stick his dick in a jar of peanut butter. The whole ordeal is unnecessarily complicated. The "actor" makes us look away while he strips naked and prepares for his big break; I try my best to keep a straight face. I adjust lights without seeing what I'm doing, and by the end of the day, the room is hot and smells of sweat and warm sandwich spread.

It doesn't take long before everyone on the substance-free floor is talking about the penis movie. The guy across the hall is famous for about five minutes. Andrew refuses to show the footage to anyone outside his film class, but the notoriety is enough to make him feel proud.

For the first time, I feel pretty good about being part of something, too.

o.

> "The glitter people know where I'm at. The gay people know where I'm at. Straight people may not know where I'm at, but they find it kind of interesting when they show up and see what is sitting around them. It's interesting to have a conglomeration of people that covers the strata from A to Z... There's a certain element of the audience that's intellectually oriented, into the lyrics... then there's another element of the audience that's into a sex trip. I'm into both of them."
> – Lou Reed, *Interview Magazine*, 1973

Though he's talking about his audience here, Lou Reed also does a bang up job in summing up art school. So much of the experience, I begin to understand, is showing up and seeing what is happening around you. There are occasions when you "know where it's at," and there are moments you're last week's big deal. The highs and lows are powerful and devastating, and they never stop. Art is fickle. Art cares little about the artist.

However, since you're part of the audience either way, you might as well enjoy the performance.

11. Goodnight Ladies

December: I strip my bed. My clothes fit in one big bag. Final grades weren't so bad, after all. That the school works on a pass/fail system probably benefits me.

Friends drop by on their way out. There are some sad goodbyes as parents linger in the shadows, like the band is breaking up, if only for a few weeks. It's time to say goodbye, bye-bye.

I head home to spend most of my time with Jen. Nothing is perfect. One semester will not transform a person. If anything, I'm more confused than ever. But I hope that when I return to school at the end of January, everything is the same.

And, generally, everything will be the same. I will still wonder if I belong. I will still be impossibly unhip and naïve. Yet within this, I will also find solid footing in filmmaking. I will accept who I am and put in the work. I will remind myself, again and again, "I am different. I am becoming an artist." I will hum Lou Reed and inch toward adulthood. I will be worthwhile.

Contributors

Shafina Ahmed is a native New Yorker and former social worker. and a Muslim-Bengali American writer/poet. She has performed in several poetry stage & TV productions with the Full Circle Ensemble; Astoria Stand Up – Harmony & Dissonance Sessions; and "Around the Fire" QPTV with Frank Robinson. She has been featured at various poetry venues in NYC such as Nuyorican Café, Union Square Slam, Great Weather Media, Wordat4F. She currently co-curates Poets Settlement monthly Reading/Poetry Series in Brooklyn, with fellow co-curators Ricardo Hernandez, Terence Degnan, and Samantha Vacca. She is currently working on a chapbook of poetry and prose.

Noah Cicero is thrity-seven years old, grew up in a small town near Youngstown, Ohio. He has lived in Oregon, California, Grand Canyon, Arizona, Seoul, South Korea and currently resides in Las Vegas, Nevada. He has a movie made of his first book called *The Human War* which won the 2014 Beloit Film Festival award for Best Screenplay. He has books translated into Turkish, Kurdish, German and Spanish. He has nine books out, his most renown are *The Human War, The Collected Works Volume 1, Bipolar Cowboy, Go to work and do your job. Care for your children. Pay your bills. Obey The Law. Buy products*, and his recent books are a book of poems called *Nature Documentary* and a book of philosophy called *Blood Soaked Buddha/Hard Earth Pascal*. He has short stories, poems, and articles published in many places.

Daniel Elder lives and writes in Portland, Oregon, with his cat Terence. His work appears in *The Rumpus, Maudlin House, Gertrude Press, Origins Journal, Nailed Magazine*, and more. He misses his mom.

Jennifer Fitzgerald Jen Fitzgerald is a poet, essayist, photographer, and a native New Yorker who received her MFA in Poetry at Lesley University and her BA in Writing at The College of Staten Island (CUNY). For 2018, Jen is the Managing Editor for the small, Los

Angeles based press, Agape Editions. She is a member of New York Writers Workshop, and teaches creative writing workshops online and around New York City. Her first collection of poetry, "The Art of Work" was published by Noemi Press in September of 2016. Her essays, poetry, and photography have appeared in such outlets as *PBS Newshour, Boston Review, Tin House, Salon, PEN Anthology, Colorado Review*, Harriet: The Poetry Foundation Blog, Best American Poetry Blog, among others. She is living in and restoring a 200 year old hotel/boarding house on Staten Island as she completes two collections.

Mark David Goodson is a writer who lives outside of Washington D.C. His blog, the Miracle of the Mundane, is a popular stop for folks in recovery from drugs and alcohol or anyone interested in the ordinariness of the extraordinary. He is currently searching for a home for his debut novel while working on several other long-term projects. If you see him, just know he'd rather be writing.

Sarah Marcus-Donnelly is the author of *They Were Bears* (2017, Sundress *Publications)*, *Nothing Good Ever Happens After Midnight* (2016, GTK Press), and the chapbooks BACKCOUNTR (2013) and *Every Bird, To You* (2013). She is an editor at **Gazing Grain Press** and the Series Editor for *As It Ought To Be's* High School Poetry Series: Gender, Identity, & Race. You can find her at www.sarahannmarcus.com.

Cory Mesler has been published in numerous anthologies and journals including Poetry, Gargoyle, Five Points, Good Poems American Places, and New Stories from the South. He has published nine novels, four short story collections, and five full-length poetry collections, and a dozen chapbooks. His novel, *Memphis Movie*, attracted kind words from Ann Beattie, Peter Coyote, and William Hjorstberg, among others. He's been nominated for the Pushcart many times, and three of his poems were chosen for Garrison Keillor's Writer's Almanac. He also wrote the screenplay for *We Go On*, which won The Memphis Film Prize in 2017. With his wife he runs a 143 year-old bookstore in Memphis. He can be found at https://coreymesler. wordpress.com.

Nicholas Powers is a poet, reporter and Associate Professor of English at SUNY Old Westbury. His book, The Ground Below Zero: 9/11 to Burning Man, New Orleans to Darfur, Haiti to Ocuppy Wall Street. He writes for Truth-Out, the Indypendent and has been interviewed by CNN.

Matthew Stephen Sirois' fiction and essays have appeared in The New Guard Review, Split Lip Magazine, Necessary Fiction, The Ghost Story, and elsewhere. His debut novel, *Near Haven*, was released in September, 2017 by Belle Lutte Press. Matthew lives in rural Massachusetts with his wife and their daughter, and works as a metal fabricator. Follow him on Twitter @matthew_sirois or visit his website at www.matthewstephensirois.com.

Erik Wennermark 's short story collection *Evil Men* is forthcoming from Run Amok Books. Find his novella "The True Story of Yu Fen" and other work online.

Benjamin Woodard is a former editor at Numéro Cinq Magazine and is currently editor-in-chief at Atlas and Alice. His fiction and nonfiction have appeared in numerous print and online journals, and his literary criticism often appears in Publishers Weekly and Kenyon Review Online. He lives and teaches in Connecticut. Find him online at benjaminjwoodard.com and @woodardwriter.

Acknowledgements

"Bellies" first appeared in *Nailed* (February 27, 2017).

"None of These Tattoos Are Mine" first appeared in *Literary Orphans* (August, 2015).

"The World is Wicked When You Grow Up as a Girl" first appeared in The Establishment (May 11, 2016).

"Island of Light, Island of Shadow" first appeared in *The Indypendent* (November 20, 2017; Issue 230).

"Brad Beckett: A Eulogy" and "On Saying Goodbye" first appeared in *Split Lip Magazine*.

"How to Cross the Street in Saigon (not to be attempted after dark)" first appeared in *[PANK]* (November 28, 2011). "Fight Privilege" first appeared in *Talking Book* (August 17, 2016). "AQI-XMAS" first appeared in *Talking Book* (December 25, 2016). "Occupy Tour Guide" first appeared in *Asian Review of Books* (January 18, 2017). "I am Willy Wonka" first appeared in *Litro* (June 6, 2017)

"Exoneration" first appeared in *5×5* (Issue 4: Outsider, May 2016). "Notes to a Turntable" first appeared in *Alternating Current* (August 2015 & 2017). "TRANSFORMER/TARNSEMOFR_R" first appeared, under the title "#194: Lou Reed, 'Transformer' (1972)," at The RS 500